# PAM GEMS

## Plays Nine

# PAM GEMS

## Plays Nine

A DOLL'S HOUSE

GHOSTS

HEDDA GABLER

AFTER BIRTHDAY

Q

QUOTA BOOKS LTD
LONDON

Published in 2022 by Quota Books Ltd.
197 Hammersmith Grove, London W6 0NP
website: www.quotabooks.com – email: info@quotabooks.com
Twitter: @Quotabooks



A CIP record for this book is available from the British Library.

ISBN 978-1-7398894-4-9

Typeset in the UK by M Rules
Printed and bound by Biddles
Picture of Pam Gems courtesy of Jonathan Gems
Cover by TRISTAN


Available from Amazon, Ingram Spark, Quota Books
and all politically correct bookstores.

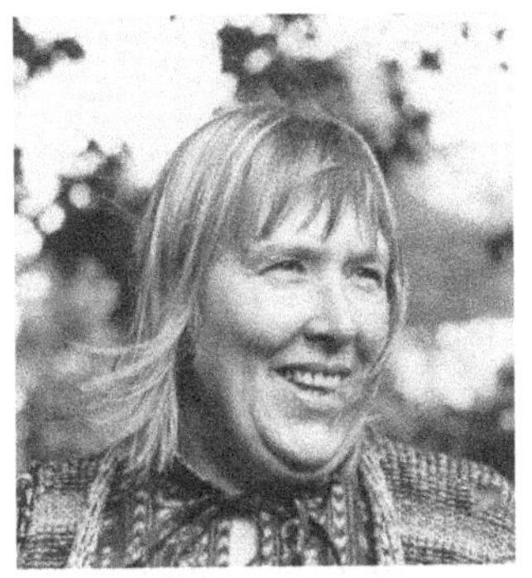

**Pam Gems** was born in 1925 in Mudeford, near Christchurch, in what was then Dorset, on the south coast of England. Her father, a Welsh ex-coalminer, died when she was six years old, leaving her mother to bring up Pam and her two brothers on her own.

For most of her childhood Pam's family lived in poverty, reliant on charity from the parish church and the Salvation Army. At eleven, she won a scholarship to grammar school, where she flourished, but left at fifteen to go to work.

World War Two broke out and, in 1943 (when she turned eighteen), she joined the Women's Royal Naval Service, and worked with British and Canadian bomber squadrons. She writes about this in FINCHIE's WAR.

After the war, she went to Manchester University, where she studied psychology and met her future husband, Keith.

Always stage-struck, Gems wrote her first play when she was eight, and was an enthusiastic participant in school plays. At university, she joined the dramatic society, wrote skits, produced and directed. After university, she worked in audience research at the BBC – which she loathed – and became part of the 'Ban the Bomb' London beatnik scene, which included Ted Hughes, the poet, Sean Kenny, the designer, and Robert Bolt, the playwright.

After marrying and having her first two children, she and her husband moved to Wandsworth in South London, where she wrote radio plays, beginning an extraordinarily prolific writing career that produced over seventy plays and adaptations. Pam Gems is, without doubt, Britain's greatest woman dramatist, with only Agatha Christie having had more West End productions.

Agatha Christie had ten plays presented in the West End, at a time when the economics of the West End plays weren't as prohibitive as they later became. Pam Gems had six, arguably seven, plays produced in the West End. The first was DUSA FISH STAS and VI, at the Mayfair, presented by Michael Codron, followed by PIAF, at the Piccadilly, presented by the RSC, which also later produced CAMILLE at the Comedy, and THE BLUE ANGEL at the Globe. LOVING WOMEN was presented at the Arts Theatre, and MARLENE had a successful run at the Lyric. STANLEY, which played to full houses at the Olivier Theatre, was offered a West-End transfer by three managements, but the company turned down these offers in favour of a transfer to the Circle in the Square, off-Broadway, in New York, where it ran for six months.

One thing that especially fascinates in the depth of Pam Gems' writing is the prophetic element. She perceived, well in advance, the dangers facing the pampered and decadent West, which we now see unfolding. As Victor Hugo said: 'Adversity makes men and prosperity makes monsters.' Her approach is always positive, however. Like the Beatles' song, all you need is love.

Jonathan Gems

# ALSO BY THE SAME AUTHOR

Betty's Wonderful Christmas

Go West Young Woman

Queen Christina

Piaf

Camille

Pasionaria

Deborah's Daughter

Marlene

Stanley

The Snow Palace

King Ludwig of Bavaria

Mrs. Pat

Ethel

Not Joan the Musical

The Socialists

Dusa, Fish, Stas, and Vi

Aunt Mary

Garibaldi, Si!

The Incorruptible

The Treat

Franz Into April

Up in Sweden

Next Please

The Synonym

The Whippet

The Russian Princess

The Burning Man

A Builder by Trade

The Nourishing Lie

Mr Watts

In Donegal

Cluster

Down West

The Country House Sale

In The Hothouse

Guin for Guinevere

Marine

The Project

You Should Be Pleased He Likes Me

What Luck

An Ordinary Woman

We Never Do What They Want

Stella Campbell

My Warren

Finchie's War

The Leg-Up

Maytime

Mabel's Bistro

A Kind of Ecstasy

Who i s Sylvia?

At the Window

Cedric and Louise

## ADAPTATIONS

Sarah B Divine!

My Name is Rosa Luxemburg

Rivers and Forests

The Odd Women

Darling Boy

Uncle Vanya

The Seagull

Yerma

The Lady from the Sea

The Cherry Orchard

The Dance of Death

The Father

Three Sisters

The Little Mermaid

Behaving Badly

Stanley's Women

## NOVELS

Mrs Frampton

Bon Voyage, Mrs Frampton

# CONTENTS

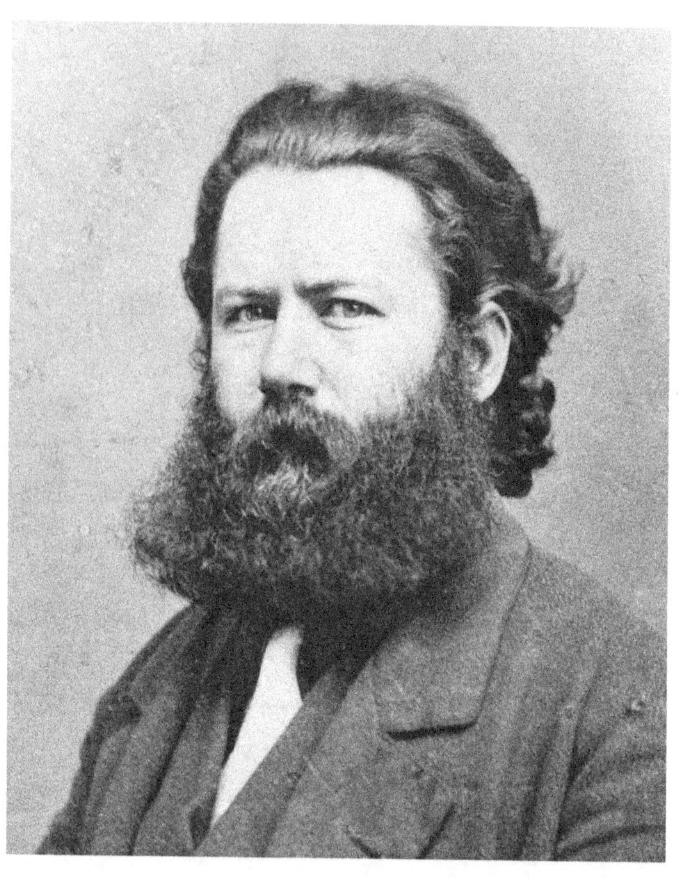

# HENRIK IBSEN

Ibsen was born on 20 March 1828 in Skien in south-east Norway, the second son of Knud Ibsen, a merchant, and his wife Marichen.

After his father became ruined, when Ibsen was about seven, the family moved to Venstope and lived in great poverty. Aged fifteen, Ibsen became an assistant to an apothecary. Later, he fathered an illegitimate child and went on to join the newly formed National Theatre of Sweden at Bergen, after writing his first play, Catiline, aged 21.

Of his early work, most of his plays were written in verse, and were failures when they opened. Later in life, he wrote his twelve great modern prose dramas, including:

| | |
|---|---|
| The Pillars of Society | 1875–77 |
| A Doll's House | 1879 |
| Ghosts | 1881 |
| An Enemy of the People | 1882 |
| The Wild Duck | 1884 |
| Romersholm | 1886 |
| The Lady from the Sea | 1888 |
| Hedda Gabler | 1890 |
| The Master Builder | 1892 |
| Little Eyolf | 1894 |
| John Gabriel Borkman | 1896 |
| When We Dead Awaken | 1899 |

# A DOLL'S HOUSE

by Henrik Ibsen

English version by Pam Gems

for Jennie Stoller

# A DOLL'S HOUSE

## by Henrik Ibsen

This version of *A Doll's House* was first presented by THE TYNEWEAR THEATRE COMPANY, on the 10th of January,1980, in Newcastle-upon-Tyne, with the following cast:

| | |
|---|---|
| Nora | GABRIELLE LLOYD |
| Torvald Helmer | DAVID BEAMES |
| Dr Rank | NICHOLAS LE PREVOST |
| Mrs Linde | JENNIE STOLLER |
| Nils Krogstad | TONY ROHR |
| Anna | NELLIE HANHAM |

| | |
|---|---|
| Directed by | RICHARD WILSON |
| Designed by | SUE MAYES |
| Lighting by | GEOFFREY MERSEREAU |
| Choreography by | JO JELLY |
| Sound by | STEFF LANGLY |
| Company Manager | BO BARTON |
| Stage Managers | LUCY ROBINSON |
| | MARK BAKER |
| | MATTHEW CLARKE |
| Artistic Director | JOHN BLACKMORE |
| Administrator | NICHOLAS JAMES |
| Production Manager | RODERICK ORR-EWING |
| Wardrobe Supervisor | GAY WILKINS |

# A DOLL'S HOUSE

A DOLL'S HOUSE, written by Henrik Ibsen in 1879, deals with the abandonment by a married woman of her husband and young children. It was an immediate succès scandale. The sound of the slamming door, as Nora left her home at the end of the play, is said to have reverberated throughout Europe.

Conventional society was shocked. How could a woman – any woman, let alone a woman of background – violate such a fundamental human law – not only of her society, but of her very sex? A female abandon her young? No mammal, human or animal, could be capable of such an act unless deranged.

The play was like a key in a door. Attention was focused on the social situation of women and their place in society. In times of rapidly increasing industry and commerce, with a concomitant need for nimble female fingers in factories and offices, such a potential source of energy began to attract serious attention.

Among the lower classes, women had always worked outside the home, in order to sustain life for themselves and their children, since a man's labouring wage was low. But, with the increase of lower managerial, office and retailing opportunities, a new kind of worker was required, and female labour acquired an enhanced commercial value. It was possible for a woman to find clean, dry, seated work, and liberation from the bondage of domestic employment – "service," as it was appropriately known. If a woman could *do*, as well as *be*, the prospects for her life were exponentially widened. Women everywhere were alerted by the possibility of new horizons – a new, unthinkable independence.

A DOLL'S HOUSE is a seminal play. Here we have a woman who has been thrust into traumatic decision by the illness of her young husband. She saves his life, at a cost to herself. Debt and secrecy dog her for years. When the truth is revealed, her husband is appalled, both by her deception and the position she has put him in. By her act, his reputation will be tarnished. Professionally, he will be ruined. He turns on his wife in recrimination and judgmental fury.

This is a revelation to her.

Like Saul on the road to Damascus, Nora's eyes are opened. She sees, for the first time, that the promise of male protection is, at best, conditional. She is shattered by Torvald's lack of fidelity and personal devotion. And she is deeply disturbed when she realises that, as a female dependent on the male hegemony, she is inadequately provided with the weapons needed, not only for contribution to society, but also for personal survival. She asks: "Who am I? Where do I stand?" And, in order to find answers, decides she must abandon her husband, her home, and her children.

Very often, with classics, productions carry the whiskers of the first exposure – understandable if there has been éclat. Thus, in A DOLL'S HOUSE, Torvald is usually played as a pompous, unimaginative bourgeois, and a bully. In fact, Torvald Helmer, is a very good husband – an attractive, hard-working and loyal partner. He is a provider and protector who adores his wife and children, and fulfils faithfully what society imposes as his role.

At a time when childbirth, and the rearing of children, were full of dangers, women with kind, effective husbands were fortunate. Even in the 1930s – fifty years later – deaths in childbirth were not infrequent. Nora had a good husband.

Productions that portray Torvald as otherwise, beg the play. Who wouldn't walk out on a humourless despot, or an unfeeling idiot? But Nora abandons her marriage in the middle of its conjugal celebration. What she gives up is *huge* and, in GHOSTS, written two years later, Ibsen continues with his theme – the need for maturation. The need for human beings to grow up.

GHOSTS is harsher on the penalties of failure to do this, and both plays are still breathtaking in their audacity.

We played this version of A DOLL'S HOUSE in Newcastle. After the first night, there was a civic reception and a discussion of the play with the aldermen's wives. At the end of the evening, there were cordial farewells. As the ladies left, one of them paused in the doorway, turned back suddenly and, bending down, whispered softly, in that wonderful Newcastle accent: "But she wouldn't have left those children, would she?" True.

Pam Gems 1980

# REVIEWS

Pam Gems's adaptation of Ibsen's century-old masterpiece (from a literal translation) does much to restore some of the thunder and lightning of its early salvoes in the cause of women's emancipation.

... Its subject is the nature of marriage – or rather, two marriages. One of the little 'songbird,' and the successful man – conventional and therefore insecure; and the other of a couple that life has treated less kindly.

Gabrielle Lloyd is successfully cast as Nora and, for that very reason, her decision to leave her husband, when the true nature of the marriage dawns upon her, is all the more impressive.

... This is an inspiring and life-enhancing play, which should not be missed. It is a bold and appropriate choice for Tyneside, the headquarters of male chauvinism, whose menfolk should be rounded up to see it, if necessary at gunpoint.

RICHARD KELLY. *The Guardian*. 12/01/1980.

In this towering adaptation by Pam Gems, Nora Helmer sloughs off the wraps of respectability to become her own person. She refuses to belong to another. Miss Gems's translation is erudite and calculating. It wrings the very last segments of humanity from Nora, and makes her a thinking woman instead of the cardboard cipher usually portrayed.

Gabrielle Lloyd plays Nora with a defined conviction; David Beames ... is a husband who resolutely demands obedience and understanding, without returning one ounce of real feeling in return. Nicholas Le Prevost's Dr. Rank is another piece of fine acting.

Sue Mayes' set is firmly middle-class...and it establishes the mood of the play completely.

PHIL PENFOLD. *The Evening Chronicle*. 11/01/1980.

All I can do here is praise, with all the authority I can muster, Pam Gems' adaptation, which is incisive and never crude, admitting an element of contemporary speech, but never swamping the feel of Ibsen himself ...

The production, by Richard Wilson, is a study in quiet excellence; deeply-layered and richly impressive.

DAVID DURMAN. *The Journal*. 11/01/1980.

# A DOLL'S HOUSE

## ACT ONE

A room, simply furnished with pale floors and bleached furniture in the Carl Larsen style. A young household, fresh and alive. The stove is lit, it is winter, Christmas time. The decorations are of live materials – fir branches, berries, and homemade ornaments of straw.

A BELL rings.

A door slams, off.

NORA enters – carrying parcels – followed by ANNA, the elderly housekeeper, who carries a Christmas tree.

> NORA
>
> Anna, quick. Hide the tree! They mustn't see it till everything's ready!

ANNA exits with the tree.

NORA, laughing, takes off her coat and hat. She finds a bag of macaroons from her coat pocket and eats one surreptitiously, as she listens at her husband's study door.

> HELMER
>
> (Within) Ahh! I think I hear a little bird in the sitting room! Or . . .

> NORA
>
> Silly! It's me!

HELMER

(*Calls*) Ohh, I thought it was a furry squirrel come to visit me.

NORA

Torvald ... (*She wipes her face free of crumbs*) ... are you busy?

HELMER

(*Looks in*) Mmm? Hullo, who's been spending again?

NORA

Come on. It's the first Christmas we haven't had to think about money all the time!

HELMER

That doesn't mean we can throw it around.

NORA

But you'll be earning heaps!

HELMER

Not until the New Year.

NORA

We can borrow till then.

HELMER

I see. And suppose a tile fell off the roof and hit me on the head?

NORA

Torvald! Don't be so dreadful! Anyway, if it did, what would I care about people wanting money? That's the last thing I'd be thinking about.

HELMER

All right, I didn't mean it. Just the same, you know how I feel about borrowing money. There'll be none of that here. Not while I'm in charge. We've managed so far. We can wait a little longer.

NORA

(*Moves away from him.*) If you say so.

HELMER follows her, and takes out his wallet.

HELMER

I do say so. Come on, I can't have my little bird sulking.

NORA

Oh! Money!

HELMER

(*Giving her banknotes.*) I know there's a lot to buy at Christmas.

NORA

Ten ... twenty ... thirty ... Torvald, thank you. This will really help!

HELMER

Good, because it's going to have to do.

NORA

Come and see what I've bought. The new suit is for Ivar. And a sword. The horse is for Bobby, and the trumpet. And look, the doll, with a doll's bed, for Emmy. They're not wonderfully special, but she'll have them all to bits soon enough.

HELMER

What's in that one?

NORA

Don't touch! Not till tonight. It's a secret!

HELMER

Aha! All right. And now that you've broken the bank,
what would <u>you</u> like?

NORA

Me? Oh nothing.

HELMER

Nothing?

NORA

Truly.

HELMER

Nonsense. There must be something you want –
within reason of course.

NORA

Not a thing.

HELMER

Come on ...

NORA

We-ell ...

HELMER

Mmm?

NORA

Well, perhaps ... No, no ...

HELMER

Come on, out with it!

NORA

Just a tiny bit more money? Just for me, to spend as I
please. I might see something I really liked.

ACT ONE

HELMER

Now Nora, I was thinking of . . .

NORA

I'd really love that! We could wrap it in gold paper
and hang it on the tree. Treasure. That would be fun
wouldn't it?

HELMER

I can't keep up with you. I don't know, money seems to
slip through your hands like water.

NORA

It's just that I've so much to do at the moment. It'll be
lovely to take my time.

HELMER

(Smiling) All right. But buy yourself a proper
present. Don't spend it on the house and then come
running to me, because there won't be any more.

NORA

Thank you!

HELMER

You're my darling girl and I love you very much, but
you cost me a lot of money.

NORA

I'm always trying to save. You want me to look nice,
don't you?

HELMER

Of course. But spending runs in your family.
Remember your father? I don't want you . . . No, all
right. Though you had a _very_ guilty look on your face.

NORA

When?

HELMER

Just now. Have you been nibbling again?

NORA

No!

HELMER

You promised. No sweets!

NORA

No, really, I haven't.

HELMER

Not even a macaroon?

NORA

Promise.

HELMER

All right. I was only teasing. I know you wouldn't tell
me a lie. Right, no more questions. You can keep your
little secrets till we light the tree.

NORA

Doctor Rank's coming?

HELMER

Of course. I've got a very good wine. I'm looking
forward to tonight. Better than last year, eh?

NORA

What?

HELMER

We hardly saw you! All those paper flowers! You were
closeted for weeks and, in the end, we didn't see them.
The cat got in and ripped them to pieces, remember?
*(He kisses her fingers)* You won't have to spoil your
poor fingers any more. Those days are over.

NORA

I still can't believe it.

HELMER

We must start making plans for next year.

The DOORBELL rings.

HELMER

Hullo, who's that? If it's for me, I'm not at home.

NORA tidies hastily as ANNA enters.

ANNA

There's a lady to see you, Miss Nora.

NORA

Oh, who? Very well, Anna, show her in.

ANNA

*(To HELMER)* Doctor Rank's here sir, he's in the
study.

HELMER

Oh, good.

HELMER exits into the study.

ANNA shows in MRS LINDE, who is wearing travelling clothes.

MRS LINDE

*(Hesitant)* Nora?

NORA

(*Not recognizing her*) How do you do?

MRS LINDE

Don't you remember me?

NORA

I'm so sorry. I'm afraid ... No, surely? No, it can't be.
Kristina? Kristina!

MRS LINDE

Yes!

NORA

Kristina, is it really you? And to think that I didn't
recognise you!

MRS LINDE

I have changed.

NORA

Well, a little ...

MRS LINDE

It's been a long time. Ten years.

NORA

Never ... no, really? That long? I suppose it must
be. Let me take your things. I've been so wrapped
up in the family. You know how it is when you're
surrounded. Everything's so busy. Time just swoops
by. When did you arrive?

MRS LINDE

I came in on the steamer this morning.

NORA

Just in time for Christmas! You'll spend it with us?
No you must. I insist. It'll be lovely! There, that's

better. Come and sit by the fire. We'll be nice and cosy.
No, no. You have the armchair. I'll sit in the rocker.
Ah, now you look like the old Kristina. It was just that
first moment. Let me look at you. You're paler than
you used to be ... a little thinner in the face ...

MRS LINDE

And a good deal older.

NORA

Only a little. Oh, my dear! I quite forgot. I'm so sorry, I
wasn't thinking.

MRS LINDE

I'm sorry?

NORA

I quite forgot. You're a widow now!

MRS LINDE

Well, yes ... three years ago.

NORA

You poor thing! We saw it in the newspapers. Do
forgive me. I meant to write, but you know how it is
with a family.

MRS LINDE

Oh, my dear, of course I understand.

NORA

No, I feel awful. It must have been dreadful for you. I
heard he didn't leave anything?

MRS LINDE

No.

NORA

And no children ...

MRS LINDE

Not even happy memories. I haven't been as lucky as
you.

NORA

How can you bear it, all on your own? I've got <u>three</u>.
They're out at the moment. Wait till you see them.
Well, anyway, I want to hear about you.

MRS LINDE

Nonsense. I've come for all your news.

NORA

No, I'm not going to be selfish, especially at
Christmas. You must tell me everything, and if
there's anything I can do. Oh, I forgot! The most
marvellous thing's happened. You'll never guess.

MRS LINDE

What?

NORA

Torvald's got the manager-ship of the Bank!

MRS LINDE

Your husband? Oh, how wonderful for you!

NORA

Isn't it marvellous? The salary's enormous. Much
more than the law. Well, Torvald will never touch
a case unless it's absolutely respectable. We simply
shan't know ourselves. We're going to have heaps!

MRS LINDE

(*Laughs*) Nora you're just the same as when we were
at school! The same little spendthrift!

NORA

You sound like Torvald. You're all wrong, as a matter
of fact. I've had to work. I've had to struggle.

MRS LINDE

How do you mean?

NORA

*(Catches herself up.)* Well, I used to do a little
sewing ... embroidery. We had some very difficult
times when I first married, you know.

MRS LINDE

Really?

NORA

Torvald was so worried about earning enough to keep
us that he took on too much. In the end, his health
broke down.

MRS LINDE

My dear, I didn't know.

NORA

It was a very bad time for us. The doctors warned
me ... if I didn't get him away, they wouldn't answer
for him.

MRS LINDE

I remember. Didn't you go to Italy?

NORA

Yes. It cost a fortune.

MRS LINDE

It must have!

NORA

Twelve hundred dollars. Nearly five thousand kroner.

MRS LINDE

Good heavens, Nora! How on earth did you manage it?

NORA

What? Oh. Well, I . . . I went to Papa, of course. Oh
Kristina, it was so awful! I should have been there
to nurse him. But with Torvald so ill! By the time we
came back from Italy, Papa was dead. I never saw him
again. It's the hardest thing I've ever had to bear.

MRS LINDE

I remember how close you were. But you were able to
save your husband, Nora. Tell me, is he well now?

NORA

Oh yes! He's splendid.

MRS LINDE

It's just that I heard your housekeeper say the doctor
had arrived.

NORA

Oh, that's Doctor Rank. He's our closest friend. He
calls every day. No, Torvald hasn't had a day's illness
since. We're all wonderfully well and happy. Oh, I'm so
awful! Here I am, going on about myself – do forgive
me. Tell me about your husband. I mean, I've always
known it wasn't a love-match. I could hardly ask you
at the time, but I've so often wondered why you did it.

MRS LINDE

My dear, I had to. What choice was there? Mother was
bedridden, you remember, and I had my two younger
brothers to think of.

NORA

And he was very well to do.

ACT ONE

**MRS LINDE**

That is what I was led to believe. Actually, his
business was not very sound. It fell away altogether
before he died. He left nothing.

**NORA**

But ... how do you manage?

**MRS LINDE**

I struggle on. I ran a small shop for a while, then a
little school. I don't seem to have had a day's rest for
the last three years. However, poor Mother went last
winter ...

**NORA**

Oh, I'm so sorry!

**MRS LINDE**

No, it was a release for her. My brothers are off my
hands now, so there aren't the same responsibilities.

**NORA**

At least you're free.

**MRS LINDE**

Yes, but I do find it empty with no-one to care for.
Anyway, I've come back. There's really so little out
in the country. And I must find something to occupy
myself and earn a living. I'd like office work, but it's
not easy to find.

**NORA**

Wouldn't that be very tiring? You look as though you
could do with a holiday.

**MRS LINDE**

My dear, I wish I could but alas, I don't have a fond
Papa to foot the bill.

NORA

Oh dear. I've said the wrong thing.

MRS LINDE

Not at all. It's me. I'm sorry. I'm not very good
company these days. It's so easy to become bitter,
and self- centered, when you live on your own. Do you
know, when you told me your good news about the
bank, all I could think was: I wonder if Nora could
help?

NORA

How do you mean?

MRS LINDE

Now that your husband ...

NORA

Oh, you mean now that Torvald is the Manager?

MRS LINDE

Forgive me. The thought did cross my mind.

NORA

But what a wonderful idea! Leave it to me. I'll mention
it when he's in a good mood. You know how it is with
men. I'll talk him round when ... I can always get him
to ... Well, you know.

MRS LINDE

Thank you so much. I didn't expect you to be so
understanding.

NORA

What are friends for?

MRS LINDE

I know, but you've never been exposed to life.

NORA

Don't be so patronising! You're like the rest of them.
None of you thinks I'm capable of anything!

MRS LINDE

Of course not. You've had three lovely children!

NORA

You think I've never suffered.

MRS LINDE

Not at all. Your husband's illness must have been very
worrying.

NORA

And I didn't tell you everything! Sssh, come closer.
I don't want Torvald to hear. Kristina you're not the
only one to save your family. You did everything you
possibly could.

MRS LINDE

I think I can say that, yes.

NORA

Well so have I! Taking Torvald away to Italy saved his
life! I arranged it. I did it.

MRS LINDE

Thank heavens it was possible.

NORA

Only because of me.

MRS LINDE

I know. You mustn't blame yourself for leaving your
father. Helping you was what he wanted.

NORA

But he didn't. He didn't help me.

MRS LINDE

What? But ...

NORA

That's what I told everyone.

MRS LINDE

But didn't you just say ... ?

NORA

We didn't get the money from Papa. I got it!

MRS LINDE

How?

NORA

By myself! Torvald doesn't know!

MRS LINDE

A sum like that? You couldn't have done!

NORA hums, tantalisingly.

MRS LINDE

You certainly couldn't have borrowed such a sum.

NORA

Why not?

MRS LINDE

Because a wife may not borrow money without the consent of her husband.

NORA

She can. If she knows where to go. Anyway, who said borrow? You said borrow. There are all sorts of ways I might have got it. After all, I'm not bad looking. Come on, you're dying to know!

**MRS LINDE**

Oh my dear. You haven't got into a mess, have you?

**NORA**

I saved my husband's life. You can hardly call that a
mess.

**MRS LINDE**

You mean he doesn't know?

NORA shakes her head.

**MRS LINDE**

Surely that was unwise? To go behind his back?

**NORA**

How could I tell him? He'd no idea how ill he was! It
was a terrible time. I couldn't go to Papa. If only he'd
been well! But I know he understands. He wouldn't
have disapproved.

**MRS LINDE**

And you're saying that you've never told your
husband?

**NORA**

I couldn't. He's terribly strict about money and, in any
case … No, it would never do.

**MRS LINDE**

Why?

**NORA**

Kristina, you know what men are like. He couldn't
bear it. Being in my debt would humiliate him. No, no.
It would upset everything.

**MRS LINDE**

Are you never going to tell him?

NORA

One day, perhaps. When I'm old and losing my looks. I
shall need something then.

MRS LINDE

Nora!

NORA

No, I'm never going to tell him. We'll keep it a secret,
just me and you.

MRS LINDE

But you still haven't told me how you managed it?

NORA

It's been the most awful struggle. If I'd known
what I was taking on. I mean, just keeping up with
the interest, let alone the instalments. It's been a
nightmare.

MRS LINDE

You mean you've been paying it back, all by yourself?

NORA

All this time.

MRS LINDE

How?

NORA

As I've discovered, it's barely possible. I save most of
my dress allowance for a start, and there are ways
of making money. Last year I got some copying. I told
Torvald I was making Christmas decorations in the
attic. It was miserable work. I thought my eyes would
fall out. Although, you know, I do enjoy the feeling of
earning my own living. I can see how men must feel.

MRS LINDE

How much have you managed to repay?

NORA

I'm not absolutely sure. It's difficult to keep a clear
account with the sliding interest. All I know is, it's
taken every penny I've laid my hands on for the
past eight years. There have been times when I was
absolutely desperate. I used to dream of a letter
arriving … you've inherited everything … he's left
you the lot!

MRS LINDE

Who? Who do you mean?

NORA

No-one. Just my dream when there seemed to be
no end to it. But not anymore! Torvald's promotion
means it's all over! I shall be able to pay up, finish!
I shall be able to buy things for the house without
cheating and skimping. I'm going to sit in the garden
and play with the children. Oh, it's so good! Think of
it. Spring isn't far off. Blue skies again! We could even
go away. Just think. A holiday!

The DOORBELL rings.

MRS LINDE

(*Rising*) I must be going.

NORA

No, no. It'll be for Torvald. Don't go.

ANNA

(*At the door*) Excuse me, Miss Nora, there's a
gentleman to see you.

NORA

Who is it?

KROGSTAD

(*At the door*) Good day, Mrs Helmer.

MRS LINDE turns, startled. She moves away abruptly.

NORA

(*Crosses and speaks to him in a low voice*) What is it?
What do you want?

KROGSTAD

To see your husband.

NORA

Why? Why my husband?

KROGSTAD

It's to do with the bank.

NORA

In what way?

KROGSTAD

We've had the announcement. That your husband is
to be the new manager.

NORA

I see.

KROGSTAD

Just a matter of dull business, Mrs Helmer.

NORA

You'll find him in the study. Pray go through.

He crosses to the study, knocks, and goes in.

NORA busies herself at the stove.

MRS LINDE

Nora, who was that man?

NORA

His name is Krogstad. He's a lawyer.

MRS LINDE

I thought I recognised the face.

NORA

Why, do you know him?

MRS LINDE

I used to. Years ago. He's changed a good deal.

NORA

I believe his marriage wasn't very happy.

MRS LINDE

Why, is he a widower now?

NORA

Yes, very much so. He has an enormous family. There, that's beginning to burn up.

MRS LINDE

What is he doing nowadays?

NORA

I'm afraid I've no idea.

DOCTOR RANK enters from the study.

RANK

(At the door) Not at all, my dear chap. I'll only be in the way. Besides, I'm going to have a chat with Nora. (He closes the door, and sees MRS LINDE) Oh I'm so sorry. It looks as though I'm in the way here too!

NORA

Not at all. Doctor Rank ... Mrs Linde.

RANK

Now that's a name I've heard before in this house!
Didn't we meet just now on the stairs?

MRS LINDE

Yes. I'm afraid I'm not very good at stairs. I take them
rather gently.

RANK

Nothing serious, I hope?

MRS LINDE

No, no. I've just been overdoing things.

RANK

You've chosen a fine time to arrive! There won't be
much of a rest with all the Christmas celebrations.

MRS LINDE

I'm afraid I've come to work rather than celebrate.

RANK

Hardly a remedy for overdoing things.

MRS LINDE

Alas one has to exist, Doctor.

RANK

Yes, that seems to be a general opinion. I can't think
why. Never mind the agony, we all want to prolong
life. I never had a patient who was any different –
even the moral invalids of this world! There's one in
there now.

MRS LINDE

(*Quietly*) You mean Krogstad? The man who was
here?

RANK

You wouldn't know him. He works at the bank.

NORA

I didn't know that. I thought he was a lawyer.

RANK

He has a small post there. Which I suspect he is
trying to hang on to. I heard him reminding Torvald
that he had his living to make. Mrs Linde, I don't
know if it's the same where you come from but, in this
town, all the rogues seem to get the safe jobs. To keep
an eye on them perhaps. I certainly don't see honest
men getting the same treatment.

MRS LINDE

Surely, we have a duty to help people when they … ?
When they need it. We must be charitable, Doctor.

RANK

Possibly. If we want to turn society into a hospital for
cripples.

NORA suddenly laughs and claps her hands.

RANK

Why, what's funny? What have you to say about
society?

NORA

Nothing, I was thinking of something else. Tell me,
are all the people at the Bank under Torvald. Will he
be in charge of everybody?

RANK

Is that what you find so amusing?

NORA

(*Smiling and humming to herself*) Yes! I do. Have a macaroon.

RANK

I thought they were forbidden fruit.

NORA

Kristina brought them for me.

MRS LINDE

What? Oh but . . .

NORA

No, no. How do you know Torvald doesn't allow them? He thinks they're bad for my teeth. However, just this once. To celebrate. There. (*She puts one in the DOCTOR'S mouth.*) Kristina. (*Gives her a macaroon.*) And one for me. Well, two. Oh, I'm so happy. In fact, there's only one thing I'd really love.

RANK

What's that?

NORA

Nothing. Just something I'd like to say to Torvald.

RANK

Then say it.

NORA

I can't, it's much too wicked.

MRS LINDE

Why, what is it?

RANK

Perhaps you'd better say it to us instead.

NORA

I couldn't!

RANK

Come on, we won't tell. What are you dying to say to
him? Come on!

He and MRS LINDE laugh.

NORA

We-ell ... what I'd really love to say is ... well I'll be
buggered!

MRS LINDE

Nora!

RANK

(Laughing) You've got your chance. Here he comes!

MRS LINDE

Really, Nora!

NORA

(Hiding the macaroons) Sssh ... Sssh!

HELMER enters, carrying his hat and coat.

RANK

Nora's got something to say to you.

NORA

Doctor, do stop it. He's only teasing. Did you manage
to get rid of ... of your visitor?

HELMER

Yes, he's gone.

NORA

Good. Let me introduce you. Kristina, this is Torvald,
my husband. This is my dear friend Kristina.
Kristina Linde. Isn't it splendid? She's coming back to
live here.

HELMER

I'm sorry, have we ...? Of course, Kristina! You grew
up together.

MRS LINDE

Yes, we're old friends.

NORA

You've heard me speak of her so often. And just think,
Torvald, she's travelled all this way especially to see
you!

HELMER

To see me?

NORA

Yes, you see, Kristina's an expert in office work. She's
looking for a post with a really able man. If she can
work under someone of real ability, she feels her work
will improve even more.

HELMER

Very sound.

NORA

So, when she'd heard you'd been made Manager of
the Bank ... You see? news gets about. You're famous
already ... She decided she couldn't miss such an
opportunity. You will be able to do something, won't
you, my love? It's in your power now. Do think about
it. Just for me ...

HELMER

Well, I shall have to consider . . .

NORA

You're bound to be making changes – choosing your
own staff. They'll expect it.

HELMER

Well, it's not impossible. I take it you're a widow, Mrs
Linde?

MRS LINDE

I am, yes.

HELMER

And you've had experience in commerce and business
matters?

MRS LINDE

Oh yes. A certain amount.

HELMER

Very well. Then it's quite possible that I may be able to
find something for you.

NORA

(Claps her hands) There . . . you see!

HELMER

You've come at a very good time, Mrs Linde.

MRS LINDE

I can't tell you how grateful I am.

HELMER

Not at all, not at all. (He puts on his coat.) And now, if
you would excuse me. I'm just on my way out.

RANK

Hang on, I'll join you. (*He gets his coat from the hall.*)

NORA

Don't be too long. Oh, are you going too, Kristina?

MRS LINDE

(*Putting on her things*) I really must. I have to find lodgings.

NORA

If only we had room here!

MRS LINDE

Nonsense. Don't think of it. You've done more than enough already. Goodbye, Nora dear. I can't begin to thank you.

They all go out into the hall.

NORA

(*Offstage*) Well au revoir for now. You'll be back this evening. No, I insist. You too, Doctor ... What do you mean, if you feel like it? ... Oh, here they are!

The sound of CHILDREN'S VOICES.

NORA

(*Offstage*) Don't they look sweet, Kristina? Look at their little cheeks. They're like apples!

RANK

(*Offstage*) Come on, it's cold!

HELMER

(*Offstage*) We'll leave her to the baby worship, Mrs Linde. No place for us, eh?

# ACT ONE

### NORA

(*Offstage*) Did you? That's a good boy! Oh Nanny, can I hold her for a minute? … I know, let's have a game. We'll play hide and seek … all right … all right? I'll hide first.

NORA runs onstage and hides under the tablecloth.

### NORA

(*Calls*) I'm ready!

KROGSTAD enters.

NORA peeps out and sees him.

### NORA

Oh.

### KROGSTAD

I beg your pardon.

### NORA

(*Getting up*) What do you want?

### KROGSTAD

The front door was open.

### NORA

My husband is out. Just a moment.

NORA Exits

### NORA

(*Offstage*) Children, go and find Nanny, I'm busy at the moment. Don't be silly. Of course he's not going to hurt us. Now run along. We'll play in a minute.

NORA returns.

### NORA

My husband …

KROGSTAD

I'd like a word with you if I may.

NORA

But it's not the first of the month! I can't give you any money now. It's not convenient.

KROGSTAD

I haven't come here for money.

NORA

Then what do you want? (*She crosses, and closes the door.*)

KROGSTAD

I saw your husband leave a moment ago.

NORA

Well?

KROGSTAD

He was with a lady.

NORA

Yes.

KROGSTAD

May I ask if her name is Linde?

NORA

Yes, it is.

KROGSTAD

She's just arrived here?

NORA

This afternoon, if you must know.

KROGSTAD

Is she a friend of yours?

NORA

As a matter of fact, she is. Though I can hardly see
that it's any concern of . . .

KROGSTAD

I used to know her.

NORA

Yes, so she said.

KROGSTAD

Oh, you know all about it? No doubt she told you.
There's something else I overheard. Tell me, is she
being offered a post at the Bank?

NORA

Mr Krogstad. May I remind you that you are now
one of my husband's subordinates. Since you are so
interested – yes. Mrs Linde has been offered a post.
On my recommendation. I hope that this satisfies you.

KROGSTAD

I knew it.

NORA

(Pacing) As you see, even a woman may have a
little influence. It might be wise, Mr Krogstad, to
remember how you are placed. I should hardly have
thought it prudent to offend those in positions of . . .
of . . .

KROGSTAD

Influence?

NORA

Exactly.

**KROGSTAD**

(*Change of voice*) Then, Mrs Helmer, since you have, as you say, so much influence, be good enough to invoke it on my behalf, if you please.

**NORA**

What do you mean?

**KROGSTAD**

I must ask you to use your influence so that I'm not put to the inconvenience of losing my 'subordinate' position at the bank, as you phrase it.

**NORA**

I wasn't aware that your position was at risk.

**KROGSTAD**

Oh please, spare me. I now see quite clearly why I've been dismissed. Since our mutual friend would no doubt find it embarrassing to work under the same roof, you've made it your business to see that I am removed, for her benefit.

**NORA**

Nonsense. Nothing like that was mentioned.

**KROGSTAD**

Yes, yes, yes of course. So you say. What is important is that there is still time for you to get me reinstated. I must ask you to do that.

**NORA**

But Mr Krogstad ... if it is true that you have, indeed, lost your position, there's nothing I can do about it.

**KROGSTAD**

Oh? But didn't you just tell me that you had influence?

ACT ONE

NORA

Yes, but that was an entirely different matter. You can't seriously suppose that my husband would take my advice on matters of business.

KROGSTAD

On the contrary, having known your husband since we were boys, I am aware that he is no less susceptible than any other man. Bank Manager or not.

NORA

I'm sorry but, if you speak of my husband like that, I shall have to ask you to leave.

KROGSTAD

Noble sentiments.

NORA

There's no need to think that I'm afraid of you, Mr Krogstad, because I'm not. Things are going to be very different in the New Year.

KROGSTAD

Now you listen to me. I need this position. What is more, I'm prepared to go to a good deal of trouble to hang on to it. Never mind how inconvenient it may be to others.

NORA

So it appears.

KROGSTAD

It's not the money. God knows that's little enough. Perhaps I should explain. I've no doubt you already know that I had a difficult time some years ago ... in business.

NORA

I have heard something about it.

KROGSTAD

Oh, I'm sure you have. A small mistake. A lapse. For
which I've been condemned, thrown out ... forced
into the sort of business that brought you to see me.
Believe me, I'm not a money-lender by choice. My post
at the bank is essential. It's a matter of reputation,
re-establishment. My sons are growing up. I've their
future to consider. To be thrown out now – just when
I've begun to hold up my head again. Another kick in
the face? No, I won't stand for it.

NORA

Mr Krogstad, there's really nothing I can do.

KROGSTAD

You're not prepared to help?

NORA

I really can't.

KROGSTAD

I see. Well if that's your attitude, I'm afraid I shall
have to force your hand.

NORA

What on earth do you mean?

KROGSTAD

You know very well what I mean. I shall be obliged to
take steps.

NORA

Steps? What steps? You mean approach my husband?

ACT ONE

KROGSTAD

If necessary.

NORA

But you can't!

KROGSTAD

I may have to.

NORA

But I can repay you now. In full! You can't. You
promised! It would be a wicked thing to do. (*Near
to tears*) You know very well that I don't want my
husband to know. It would spoil everything!

KROGSTAD

I'm afraid ...

NORA

... and hearing it from you. No, it would be so
unpleasant!

KROGSTAD

Have you quite finished?

NORA

You horrible man! Go on – tell him! See if you keep
your job then! You didn't think of that, did you?

KROGSTAD

And you seem to be under a few misapprehensions.
You really believe that, if the truth were told, there
would be no more than a little unpleasantness?

NORA

What do you mean? If you tell my husband, he will
simply pay you what is outstanding, and we shall be
sure to have nothing further to do with you.

KROGSTAD

Ah, Mrs Helmer, if only it were so simple.

NORA

What do you mean?

KROGSTAD

Either my memory has failed me, or you have an even
poorer head for business than I thought. Let me make
things a little plainer for you.

NORA

I don't understand.

KROGSTAD

Oh, you will. At the time of your husband's illness, you
borrowed twelve hundred dollars from me.

NORA

Only because I was desperate.

KROGSTAD

I raised the money against your own note of hand.

NORA

Which I signed.

KROGSTAD

Exactly. With your father as guarantor.

NORA

Yes.

KROGSTAD

His signature too.

NORA

Yes.

KROGSTAD

And there was a space for the date for your father
to fill in when he appended his signature, is that not
correct?

NORA

Yes, I think so. I don't remember.

KROGSTAD

And I gave the document to you, to post to your
father, is that not the case?

NORA

Yes.

KROGSTAD

Which you returned to me, five or six days later, with
your father's signature.

NORA

That is so.

KROGSTAD

And you received the money.

NORA

Yes! What's all this about? I've kept up the payments
haven't I . . . ?

KROGSTAD

More or less. Your father, I believe, was ill at the time.

NORA

My father, Mr Krogstad, was dying.

KROGSTAD

That is so. He died soon after, did he not?

NORA

Yes.

KROGSTAD

You remember the date of course?

NORA

September the 29th.

KROGSTAD

Precisely. I took the trouble to remind myself. Which brings us to something rather curious. (*He produces a paper.*)

NORA

I don't understand.

KROGSTAD

I have often wondered, Mrs Helmer, how it was that your father signed this guarantee against your debt three days after he died.

NORA does not reply.

KROGSTAD

Can you explain that? Something else. When I came to examine the date, I thought I recognised the handwriting. It's quite possible, of course, that your father forgot to add the date and that someone else wrote it in for him. But it did make me take another look at the signature. That, after all, is what matters. What is of vital importance is the signature. I am speaking, of course, of the absolute necessity for your father to have signed the document himself. It has occurred to me to wonder. Did he, in fact, do so? Is the signature itself genuine? Or did ... perhaps ... someone else sign ... ?

NORA

I signed it.

KROGSTAD

(*After a pause*) That statement, I am bound to say, constitutes a very dangerous admission.

NORA

(*Slight pause*) I can't in the least see why. You'll have the rest of the money soon enough.

KROGSTAD

You didn't send the paper to your father, did you?

NORA

No.

KROGSTAD

But why in heaven's name not?

NORA

He was dying! How could I bother him for money? How could I tell him that my husband's life, too, was in danger? I had to take certain decisions. I could at least save one of my beloveds by taking him to a warmer climate.

KROGSTAD

It might have been a great deal wiser, in retrospect, to have abandoned the idea.

NORA

I saved his life!

KROGSTAD

By dishonesty.

NORA

Nonsense.

KROGSTAD

Did you realise that you were defrauding me?

NORA

My husband was desperately ill! Your only concern was to make profit out of the situation! Do you think I cared about you?

KROGSTAD

Obviously not! But there's something you should know. What you did to me was no more, no less than the slip that I made in a similar business transaction, which has ruined my name, my reputation and my career. The very same thing.

NORA

But did you do it to save someone's life? What was your motive?

KROGSTAD

Oh, the law is not concerned with motive.

NORA

That's ridiculous. Then the law is useless!

KROGSTAD

Useless or not, it is the law that you will be judged by, if I produce this piece of paper before a court.

NORA

You mean the law doesn't allow a daughter to protect a dying father? That it doesn't allow a wife to save her husband's life? If that's the law … no, I don't believe it. Nobody could be so cruel. I suggest you learn a little more about your own profession, Mr Krogstad.

KROGSTAD

Believe what you wish, I know what I'm talking about.
I know exactly where I stand in relation to this.
*(He waves the paper)* And I know where you stand.
I've made myself perfectly clear. If I am to lose my
position, and everything I've been working for, then
you must be prepared to take the consequences. I've
no intention of going down a second time when it is in
your power to prevent it.

NORA

But there is nothing I can do!

KROGSTAD

That must be your decision. But let me make
something clear. If I go down, I shall make it my
business to take you with me. Make no mistake about
that.

KROGSTAD exits.

NORA

Oh, what rubbish! He's trying to frighten me! *(She
begins to tidy.)* How can it be wrong?

CHILD

*(Offstage)* Mummy, are you coming?

NORA

*(Calls)* Not just now, darling.

CHILD

*(Off)* Has the man gone?

NORA

*(At the door)* Yes, but let's keep it a secret. We won't
tell anyone, mmm? Not even Daddy. Run along,
Mummy's got a lot to do. *(She closes the door, picks*

up a piece of embroidery, and puts it down.) No, it's impossible. Anna, could you bring in the tree now? (She finds the tree decorations.)

ANNA enters with the tree.

ANNA

Where shall I put it, Miss Nora?

NORA

Let's have it over here.

ANNA

Do you need anything else?

NORA

No, I've got everything, thank you.

ANNA goes.

NORA begins to decorate the tree. She fixes on the candles.

NORA

Now the flowers ... that horrible man ... what nonsense! I'm not going to think about it. We're all going to have a lovely Christmas together.

TORVALD enters, with papers under his arm.

NORA

You weren't long.

HELMER

Did you have a visitor?

NORA

No.

HELMER

I thought I saw Krogstad by the gate.

NORA

Oh yes. He did look in for a minute.

HELMER

I see. I see! He wanted you to put in a good word for
him? Nora! I can tell by the look on your face. It's no
good trying to hide things from me.

NORA

He did mention something.

HELMER

So that's it. Creeping in here behind my back. It was
all supposed to come from you, I daresay. Did he
suggest that as well?

NORA

Well yes, but . . .

HELMER

My dear girl! How could you listen to a man like
that . . . and lie to me on top of it!

NORA

Lie?

HELMER

Nora, you looked me straight in the face and said that
no-one had called. I can't have my own love telling
me lies. I was right, wasn't I? I thought so. Bless
you, you're my soft-hearted girl. We'll say no more
about it. (*He sits by the stove.*) Ahh, it's so warm and
comfortable in here.

He looks at his papers. NORA works on the tree.

NORA

Torvald?

HELMER

Yes?

NORA

I can't think what to wear.

HELMER

Mmm?

NORA

For the Stenborgs fancy dress party.

HELMER

You'll think of something.

NORA

It all seems rather pointless ... usually I enjoy it. (*She crosses behind him.*) Are you very busy?

HELMER

Documents from the Bank. They've allowed me to start. I'd like to get up to date before the New Year.

NORA

Tell me ... why is poor Krogstad ...

HELMER

Mmm?

NORA

(*Stroking his hair*) You know, if you weren't so dreadfully busy, I'd ask you a favour.

HELMER

What might that be?

NORA

You have such splendid taste, I wondered if you'd choose for me.

HELMER

Choose? What?

NORA

My costume, for the dance. You have such wonderful
ideas.

HELMER

We'll see. I daresay I shall come up with something.

NORA

Oh that's lovely. I knew you would! (*She goes back to
the tree.*) What did Krogstad do?

HELMER

(*Looks up*) He forged a signature.

NORA

Is that so bad?

HELMER

It's a criminal offence.

NORA

But there might have been a good reason for it.

HELMER

Possibly. More likely he just took a chance. It happens
all the time. It wasn't just that.

NORA

How do you mean?

HELMER

Any man can make a slip, be tempted in a crisis. I
wouldn't necessarily condemn him out of hand.

NORA

Of course you wouldn't!

HELMER

It wasn't quite so simple with our friend Krogstad.

NORA

Why?

HELMER

He tried to lie his way out of it. He deceived his own
family, his own children. What sort of effect do you
think that's had on them?

NORA

How do you mean?

HELMER

Nora if you expose children to an atmosphere of
lies and deception, you contaminate them. They're
corrupted from the start.

NORA

You can't mean that. Are you sure?

HELMER

I've seen it so often in my years as a lawyer. I doubt if
I've ever met a young criminal who didn't have a bad,
lying sort of woman behind him. Criminals are made
by bad mothers.

NORA

Why only mothers?

HELMER

My dear girl, who rear the children? Women! It's a
tremendous responsibility. Not that a man can't be a
bad influence too. No, that fellow Krogstad poisoned
the air in his own home. I'm sorry for his family, the
man's an untouchable. Which is why, my love ... (*He
holds out a hand to her.*) ... you mustn't ask me to

keep him on. I couldn't have him on the premises, it makes me feel physically ill just to be near such people.

NORA

(*Moving away*) Heavens, it's hot in here!

HELMER

I'm going to try and finish before dinner. (*Moving to the study.*) I'll think about your costume. Oh, and what else? I know! I'll hang a little gold package on the tree. I wonder who for! (*He caresses her.*) My little bird.

HELMER goes into the study, and closes the door.

NORA

No ... it's not true. It can't be ... it's impossible.

ANNA appears at the nursery door.

ANNA

May the children come in, Miss Nora? They've been asking very nicely.

NORA

What? Oh no, they mustn't! Don't let them in, Nanny. Keep them with you. You must look after them!

ANNA

I beg your pardon? Very well, if you say so.

ANNA goes.

NORA

Poison my own home? Corrupt my own children? I couldn't do that. How could I? How can that be true? It's not true!

*Fade to black.*

## ACT TWO

The same interior.

The Christmas tree is in the corner, its candles burnt down. NORA is alone.

NORA

Who is it? *(She listens)* There's nobody there. Who'd come on Christmas Day? Or any day? I wonder if ... *(She hurries out to the hall, and returns at once.)* Nothing in the letter box. Oh, it's silly, of course he didn't mean it. He was upset. He's not going to do anything. Good heavens, I'm the mother of three children!

ANNA enters with a large box.

ANNA

I've found them. The dressing up clothes.

NORA

Oh, put them on the table.

ANNA

They're in an awful state.

NORA

I wish I could tear them to bits.

ANNA

Heavens it's not as bad as that! We'll manage something.

NORA

I'll run to Mrs Linde's lodgings. Ask her to help.

ANNA

Now Miss Nora, you're not going out in this weather. You'll catch your death.

NORA

I daresay the world would manage without me if I did.

ANNA

Now that's silly.

NORA

How are the children? What are they doing? Are they asking for me?

ANNA

They're playing with their Christmas presents. Poor little things. They're not used to not seeing you.

NORA

Nanny, I'm not going to be able to be with them so much.

ANNA

I see.

NORA

Not in the same way. Not so close.

ANNA

(*Sighs*) Well, I suppose young children can get used to anything if they have to.

NORA

Even if I went away altogether?

ANNA

Miss Nora, whatever do you mean?

# ACT TWO

NORA

Nanny, there's something I must ask you. I've always
wanted to know.

ANNA

What?

NORA

Come and sit down.

ANNA

Now what's the matter?

NORA

How could you do it?

ANNA

Do what?

NORA

How could you bear it? Leaving your little girl with
strangers as you did.

ANNA

(*Slight pause*) Oh that. Well I had to, didn't I? I
wouldn't have been able to look after my Miss Nora,
otherwise.

NORA

But could you bear it? It must have been so hard. You
couldn't have wanted to!

ANNA

A poor girl who's got herself into trouble hasn't much
choice. I was lucky. I got the offer of a good place.
(*Low*) The man just ran off and left me to it.

NORA

But to have to give her away. Your own daughter!
(*Slight pause*) Do you ever think of her?

ANNA

Oh yes. All the time.

NORA

But surely . . . she'll have forgotten all about you by
now?

ANNA

Oh no! No, no. She's written to me . . . twice! Once when
she was confirmed, and again when she got married. I
keep the letters in my box.

NORA

Oh Nanny . . .

She puts her arms around ANNA.

NORA

Dear Nanny, you've been such a wonderful mother to
me.

ANNA

My poor girl, I was the only mother you had.

NORA

And I know that if my poor babies ever found
themselves . . . Well I know you would . . . Oh my
goodness. What nonsense I'm talking. You'd better see
what they're up to. I must think about making myself
nice for tomorrow.

ANNA

Oh, there won't be anyone as lovely as my Miss Nora!

ANNA goes.

NORA begins to unpack the box. She pauses.

> NORA
>
> Stop it. Of course he's not coming. Perhaps he'll send a
> letter. Don't be such a <u>fool</u>! Nothing's going to happen.
> Stop thinking about it. Ah, my pretty gloves. *(She
> puts down the gloves, picks up a fur muff, and strokes
> it against her cheek.)* Now stop it. Stop thinking!

There is a KNOCK at the door.

NORA jumps, with a little scream.

MRS LINDE enters, tapping the inner door as she enters.

> NORA
>
> Oh, it's you, Kristina! I thought it was somebody else.
> Come in, come in. Thank you so much for coming.

> MRS LINDE
>
> They said you'd called.

> NORA
>
> Come and sit on the sofa. I've a favour to ask you.

> MRS LINDE
>
> My dear, anything.

> NORA
>
> The Stenborgs upstairs are giving a fancy dress.
> They do it every year. Torvald wants me to go as a
> Neapolitan fisher-girl, and dance the tarantella. I
> learned it when we were in Capri.

> MRS LINDE
>
> What a lovely idea!

NORA

Oh well, it's his idea. This is the costume. He had it made for me when we were there, but it's in a dreadful state.

MRS LINDE

Let me see. (*She picks up the dress.*) It's mostly the trimming that's come away.

NORA

You were always so good with a needle ...

MRS LINDE

Have you a sewing box? Ah ...

NORA gives it to her.

MRS LINDE

Thank you. That's all I'll need.

NORA

Oh Kristina, thank you so much!

MRS LINDE

(*Sitting*) May I drop in tomorrow and see you in all your finery?

NORA

Of course!

MRS LINDE

(*Sewing*) I did enjoy last evening. Thank you for a lovely time.

NORA

What? Oh ... yes. It wasn't as much fun as usual ... no ... Yes, Torvald is so good at running things and making everyone comfortable.

**MRS LINDE**

You, too, Nora. You're not your father's daughter for nothing. Tell me, is Doctor Rank always so quiet?

**NORA**

Mmmm?

**MRS LINDE**

He seemed a little depressed, I thought.

**NORA**

Poor man. He's terribly ill, you know. It's his spine.

**MRS LINDE**

How awful! Has he any dependents?

**NORA**

No, he's all on his own.

**MRS LINDE**

He looks well to do. Is he?

**NORA**

Oh yes, very. He's never been strong. They say it's all because his father led a certain sort of life – you know, with women.

**MRS LINDE**

(*Puts down her sewing*) Nora, what on earth do you know of such matters?

**NORA**

I have had three children! You pick things up, talking to the monthly nurse. Women do talk.

**MRS LINDE**

(*Resumes her sewing*) Does he call every day?

NORA

Doctor Rank? Oh yes, he never misses.

MRS LINDE

He seemed to know all about me. I suppose he was
being gallant. Mr Helmer obviously had no idea who
I was.

NORA

That's because I don't talk to Torvald about my old
friends. He gets so jealous and possessive. With
Doctor Rank, I talk away like a house on fire.

MRS LINDE

My dear. Do forgive me, but it might be wiser to be
just a little more discreet.

NORA

What do you mean? What on earth are you talking
about?

MRS LINDE

Doctor Rank.

NORA

I don't understand.

MRS LINDE

When you were talking about your rich admirer the
other day.

NORA

Kristina! I was just imagining! There's nobody
real … More's the pity!

MRS LINDE

I see. You say he's very well off?

NORA

Oh yes, very.

MRS LINDE

And he calls every day?

NORA

Yes, why not?

MRS LINDE

I'm surprised that a man of his breeding has so little
discernment.

NORA

What do you mean?

MRS LINDE

Oh Nora, please. We're old friends. It's obvious where
you got the money. The money to go abroad – the
twelve hundred dollars.

NORA

From Doctor Rank? I wouldn't dream of such a thing.
He's a friend of the family. How could you think such
a thing? Imagine, with his calling every day!

MRS LINDE

So it wasn't him?

NORA

No, of course not. In any case, he wasn't a rich man
then. He inherited much later.

MRS LINDE

Well, thank goodness for that.

NORA

Mind you, he's such a dear that if ever I . . .

MRS LINDE

Oh, but you wouldn't. Not behind your husband's back?

NORA

No, no, no. I've done that once. That's quite enough to be worrying about.

MRS LINDE

Men are so much better placed to deal with these things.

NORA

I quite agree. Oh, what nonsense it all is! Tell me something. When you're repaid a debt in full your bond is returned to you, that's right, isn't it?

MRS LINDE

Oh yes.

NORA

So you can tear the beastly thing up?

MRS LINDE

(Looks at her hard) Nora, is there something you haven't told me?

NORA

Is it as plain as all that?

MRS LINDE

What's the matter? Has something happened? Tell me.

NORA

(Crosses to her) Kristina. (She listens.) Ssh . . . it's Torvald. Could you pop into the nursery with the sewing? You'll find Nanny there with the children.

Only Torvald hates to see dressmaking about the place. He grumbles.

MRS LINDE

Of course.

NORA

Nanny can give you a hand.

MRS LINDE

All right, but we must have a talk later. I'm not going till you tell me.

She takes the dress and sewing box and goes.

TORVALD enters from within. NORA joins him.

HELMER

Was that the dressmaker?

NORA

No, it's Kristina.

HELMER

Oh, what does she want?

NORA

She's helping me with my costume for tomorrow. I'm going to look splendid.

HELMER

And whose idea was it? And a very good one, though I say so myself.

NORA

And who's a nice, obedient girl?

HELMER

Now squirrel, obeying your husband is not to be thought of as out of the ordinary. All right, all right,

I know you're only teasing. Off you go. You'll want to try everything on I suppose, eh?

NORA

You mean you've got work to do, Torvald?

HELMER

Yes?

NORA

If your little squirrel were to ask for something very, very nicely, do you think you might say yes?

HELMER

That would depend on what it was.

NORA

Your little squirrel would do nice things for you.

He laughs.

NORA

All sorts of things ... things you like very much ...

HELMER

All right, out with it. I say, it's not about Krogstad is it?

NORA

Darling, please! Just for me.

HELMER

You're not _still_ on about that?

NORA

Torvald please ...

HELMER

Nora, I'm astonished that you bring the matter up.
I've made it quite clear to you. The answer is no. Now
that's enough.

NORA

But you can't dismiss him!

HELMER

I've already given his post to Mrs Linde. I thought
you realised that.

NORA

Yes, yes, I know. And it was sweet of you. But why
not keep the poor man? You could as easily dismiss
someone else. After all, he is a widower.

HELMER

Now Nora, stop being stubborn. Just because you
were silly enough to make some sort of promise to the
wretched fellow, I'm supposed to …

NORA

Torvald, it's not because of that. It's … Well, do you
remember telling me about the pieces he sometimes
writes for the newspapers? Didn't you once say he
was a journalist? If you were to upset him, he might
write about you. And, with this new post so much in
the public eye … The thought of your being exposed
in any way frightens me.

HELMER

Ah, I see! Now I understand.

NORA

What?

HELMER

My poor little worm. You're thinking of your father.

NORA

What? Oh, yes. Remember all the dreadful things
they wrote about Papa? It was such an awful
time. I don't know what we should have done if
the Ministry hadn't sent you. You were so gentle
and understanding, my darling. Oh, we mustn't go
through all that again. Give him something to do.
Just for peace and quiet. You'll have so much on your
plate, why antagonize him?

HELMER

My dear girl, what are you talking about? It's not
the same thing at all. Your father got himself into
the devil of a mess. It was as well for him that I
was so warmly disposed towards your family. This
situation's completely different. My own reputation is
entirely intact and, believe me, I intend that it shall
remain that way. So, don't ask me to do something
irregular.

NORA

But people are so horrid. Why risk it? Why spoil
everything? Torvald please ... Please do it for me!

HELMER

Nora, stop it. I'm sorry if you've got yourself into a
state, but can't you understand? Simply by asking
such a thing, you make it impossible. All I need is for
it to get about that the new manager is in his wife's
pocket!

NORA

Does that matter?

HELMER

Oh no, not at all. Just so long as my little rabbit gets
her own way! Never mind that I'm made a laughing
stock, with the whole town saying I'm easily led,
and hide behind a woman's skirts. Believe me, I
wouldn't last very long. Look, Krogstad's dismissal
has nothing to do with Mrs Linde's being offered a
post. He was going in any case. There was never any
question of my allowing him to stay.

NORA

But why?

HELMER

He's not sound. How could I employ such a man? Well,
I suppose I could ...

NORA

Yes?

HELMER

No, it's not only his reputation ...

NORA

But if you could give him a chance. Be generous ...

HELMER

It's not only that. In fact, he's rather good at his job.
But no, I can't. It's impossible.

NORA

Why?

HELMER

The fact is, we were at school together. It makes it
awkward.

NORA

Why?

HELMER

He's too familiar. He will call me by my Christian
name. It's true we were close at school, but things are
different now. He should have the decency to realise
that. But no. Every time I go through the door, it's
"Good morning, Torvald." Torvald this – Torvald that.
It makes my position intolerable.

NORA

But surely, you're not dismissing him because of
that? Take away a man's livelihood because ... Oh
Torvald, it's so petty!

HELMER

Petty, what do you mean, petty? Oh, you think I'm
petty? Is that what you think of me?

NORA

No, of course not, it's just that ...

HELMER

Not at all. If my reasons are petty, then I must be
petty. I see. Very well, since I'm petty, we'll settle the
matter once and for all. (*He calls*) Anna!

NORA

What are you doing?

HELMER

We'll see if I'm the sort to be led by a woman!

ANNA enters.

HELMER

Anna, be so good as to find a messenger for this letter.
Tell him I want it delivered at once if you please. Hang
on. I'll give you the money myself.

ANNA

Yes sir.

ANNA exits with the letter.

HELMER

So much for you, Miss Stubborn. (*Picks up his
papers.*)

NORA

Torvald, what was in it? What was in the letter?

HELMER

Krogstad's dismissal. In writing.

NORA

Torvald, call her back, quick, run after her! Get
it back. Please, for my sake. For all of us. For the
children! Please! Listen! You don't know what it will
do to us!

HELMER

Nora. The matter is over. In any case, she'll have
given it to a messenger by now. It's too late.

NORA

Yes. It's too late.

HELMER

Nora, my dear girl, you've got yourself all upset about
this. You don't think I'm going to be intimidated
by a nasty scribbler, do you? I should be insulted if
you thought that. Now, squirrel, leave things to me,

and stop worrying. I'd be a poor sort of husband if I couldn't take care of you all, eh? It's _my_ job to take the decisions and solve all the crises. I wouldn't be a man otherwise. Whatever happens, _I_ take the responsibility.

NORA

About what? What do you mean?

HELMER

Now, now ...

NORA

Nothing's going to happen. I won't let it. But if it does, I shall share the ...

HELMER

Yes, yes, we'll face it together. Will that do for you, my frightened little rabbit? It's just your woman's imagination. I tell you what, why don't you go over your steps for the dance with the tambourine? You'll need some rehearsal. Don't worry about the noise. I shan't hear you with the door closed. You won't disturb me. Oh, by the way, send the Doctor in when he comes.

He exits into the study. Pause.

NORA

He'll do it, I know he will! He meant it. There must be something! There must be some way I can ...

A KNOCK.

She pulls herself together, goes to the door, and lets in DOCTOR RANK.

NORA

Hullo! I recognised your knock. Come in, Torvald's just finishing something in the study.

During the next scene, the light fades slowly.

RANK

And what about you?

NORA

I've always time for a chat with my favourite doctor.

RANK

(*Sitting*) You know, talking to you is a particular pleasure that I shall continue to treasure ... for as long as I can.

NORA

(*Only half listening.*) As you can?

RANK

Which, I'm sorry to have to say, may not be all that long.

NORA

(*Still abstracted*) Oh?

RANK

I've had some bad news, Nora.

NORA

(*Jumps, alarmed*) News, what news? What have you heard?

RANK

(*Quietly*) I'm afraid I'm not in a very good way.

NORA

I'm sorry, what did you say?

RANK

It's just that . . . I don't think I shall be with you for
very much longer.

NORA

Oh, it's about you!

RANK

Why? What did you think I meant? I must say it's an
odd feeling to be the sickest patient on my own books.
I've been making up the accounts, as it were. As far
as my health is concerned, I appear to be more or less
bankrupt.

NORA

I don't understand.

RANK

No more time, it seems.

NORA

How long?

RANK

A month perhaps.

NORA

A month! (*Slight pause*) You can't mean it.

RANK

It's such a strange experience. I find it quite
impossible to imagine, let alone accept, the fact that,
in a month from now, I shall be rotting under the
earth in that churchyard. So odd.

NORA

Don't. Don't say such horrible things!

RANK

Yes. Pretty disgusting. And I'm afraid it's going to get worse. There is one more test to be done. I fancy it'll give me a more precise idea as to how long I've got. Look, I want you to do something for me.

NORA

Anything.

RANK

Nora, I don't want him coming to visit me.

NORA

Torvald? Why not?

RANK

He's not the man for it. We both know how squeamish he is. He doesn't have your strength. He'd hate it. When I've ... ah ... when I know how things stand I'll ... I'll let you know. I'll drop in a visiting card with a cross on it. Just to warn you to keep him away.

NORA

But ...

RANK

You know he can't bear anything ugly or unpleasant.

NORA

Oh you're being ridiculous. I won't believe you. You're in one of your funny moods. I won't listen. Just when I wanted you in a good humour.

RANK

I'm dying, Nora. And uselessly ... before my time ... for someone else's sins. It doesn't help – though I daresay I'm far from unique.

NORA

(*Covers her ears*) No, stop it, I'm not going to listen.
You're talking nonsense. Come on, do cheer up.

RANK

Well ... why not? There's a joke in it somewhere.
My father has a good time as a subaltern and my
unsuspecting spine foots the bill.

NORA

You mean for his addiction to asparagus?

RANK

And truffles, of course.

NORA

Oh, we mustn't forget the truffles. Oysters too, I
expect?

RANK

Oh oysters, certainly, by no means forget the oysters.

NORA

Wine, champagne ... all so tasty!

RANK

What a nuisance that they attack the spine.
Particularly when the spine in question hasn't had
any of the fun.

NORA

That's <u>most</u> unfair!

He gives her a searching look.

RANK

Hmmm ...

NORA

Now why are you smiling like that?

RANK

No, no, you were the one who laughed.

NORA

You laughed first!

RANK

You're a great deal naughtier than I thought. How surprising.

NORA

Nonsense, I'm in a silly mood today.

RANK

So it would seem.

NORA

Dear, dear Doctor Rank. Please don't die. You mustn't. What would we do without you?

RANK

You'll get over it soon enough. Absent friends are soon forgotten.

NORA

Do you really believe that?

RANK

Oh yes, there'll be others. Mrs Linde for example.

NORA

I hope you're not jealous of poor Kristina.

RANK

Indeed I am. She's beginning to take my place already.

NORA

Sssh, she's in the next room.

RANK

Well there you are. She's here again!

NORA

Only to help me with my costume for the dance. You are being silly. If you promise to be really nice I'll give you a special treat. I'll dance just for you tomorrow. Well, and for Torvald, of course. *(She starts to look into the box.)* Come and look. I've got something to show you.

RANK

Oh, what?

NORA

Come and see.

RANK

Mmm. Silk stockings.

NORA

Aren't they delicious? Silk. Flesh-coloured. Don't you think they're nice? Of course, it's too dark to see them properly. You must wait till tomorrow. No, no, you can only look at the feet. We-ell, perhaps if you're very good. *(She extends the stockings under his nose.)*

RANK

Very, very nice.

NORA

Why are you looking at me like that? Don't you think they'll fit?

RANK

I'm hardly in a position to judge, or form a reliable
diagnosis.

NORA hits him lightly in the face with the stockings.

NORA

You deserved that.

RANK

Have you any other pretty things to show me?

NORA

Certainly not. You've been much too bad. *(She hums
to herself, sorting through her bits and pieces.)*

RANK

*(After watching her)* What would I have done without
this house?

NORA

Yes, I really do believe you feel at home here.

RANK

When I sit talking to you like this – the two of us
together, so ... the thought of leaving ... of not being
here anymore. How can I express the gratitude I feel
towards you?

NORA

Of course you'll be here.

RANK

Dear Nora, what can I do for you?

NORA

Nothing! Perhaps ... suppose I were to ask you for
something? No, no, it doesn't matter.

RANK

Ask me for what?

NORA

Some ... proof of your friendship.

RANK

My dear, if you would just give me the opportunity.

NORA

But you don't know what it is.

RANK

Why not tell me?

NORA

Oh, but I can't. It's something enormous. I don't just mean advice. It's everything ... help, advice ... a really enormous favour.

RANK

The bigger the better, believe me. Tell me. No, please. Surely you trust me?

NORA

More than anyone in the world. You're my best friend. All right, I will tell you. It's something I have to stop, and I need your help. You know how much Torvald loves me. He would lay down his life for me.

RANK

Nora, do you think he's alone in that?

NORA

(She starts slightly) What?

RANK

Do you really think that he's the only man who would gladly die for you?

NORA

(*Sadly*) Oh. Oh, I see.

RANK

I promised myself that I would tell you. I wanted you
to know before – well, before I ... Well, now you know.
So, as you see, there is nothing I wouldn't ... I am
devoted to you.

NORA

(*In a calm voice*) Let me go, please.

She rises.

RANK

Nora ...

NORA

(*At the door, calls*) Anna, would you bring in the
lamps? (*She crosses to the stove*) Oh, what a pity. I do
so wish you hadn't done that.

RANK

Is it so terrible, to love you as others do?

NORA

Loving is one thing. Speaking of it is another.

RANK

You mean you've been aware of it?

ANNA enters with the lamps, bobs and goes.

RANK

Nora, did you know?

NORA

What does it matter? You've spoilt it. How could you be so clumsy? Just when everything was going so well.

RANK

At least you know there's nothing I wouldn't do for you.

NORA

Which you've now made completely impossible.

RANK

Why?

NORA

How can I?

RANK

Don't punish me. That would be cruel. Ask anything of me. If it's humanly possible, you shall have it.

NORA

Oh, I've been talking nonsense. It's just some silliness. Let's forget all about it. No really, I mean it! *(She sits by him, smiling)* Just the same, you're a fine one! Aren't you ashamed of yourself, now the lamp's lit?

RANK

No. But would you like me to say goodbye? Would you rather I didn't call again?

NORA

Of course you must come. You know how I love to see you. We have enormous fun.

RANK

Yes. You know, you've always been a mystery to me.
I'd swear you enjoy my company more than his.

NORA

Surely it's possible to love someone but to prefer the
company of someone else?

RANK

I suppose that's possible.

NORA

When I was at home, naturally I loved Papa best. Just
the same, it was much nicer being with the servants.
For one thing, they didn't preach at me all the time,
and they were such fun to gossip with.

RANK

I see. So I've taken their place?

NORA

Of course not. I didn't mean it like that. It's just that,
sometimes, living with Torvald is a little like living
with Papa. If you see what I mean.

ANNA enters with a visiting card.

ANNA

Excuse me, Miss Nora, excuse me, Doctor. (*She hands
the card to NORA, whispers in her ear. NORA looks
quickly at the card.*)

NORA

Oh! (*She pockets the card quickly.*)

RANK

Is something wrong?

NORA

No, no, nothing. It's just ... it's just about my costume
for the ball.

RANK

But isn't it over there?

NORA

Yes ... no ... This is another one. I don't want Torvald
to know about it.

RANK

I see. So that's the great secret!

NORA

Ye-es! Do you think you could go and keep him
occupied for a while?

RANK

Don't worry. I'll bar the door if necessary.

DR RANK goes into Torvald's study.

NORA

(*To ANNA*) Where is he?

ANNA

In the kitchen. He came in the back way.

NORA

Didn't you tell him that I wasn't at home? That I had
a visitor?

ANNA

I tried, Miss Nora, but he won't go. He says he wants
to see you.

NORA

Oh, very well. You'd better bring him in. Anna ...

ANNA

Yes, Miss Nora?

NORA

I don't want this mentioned to Mr Helmer.

ANNA nods and goes.

NORA

Oh God! It's going to happen. No, I won't let it, I shan't
let it ... ! (*She crosses to the study and quietly bolts
the door.*)

KROGSTAD enters, heavily dressed against the cold.

NORA

I must ask you to keep your voice down, my husband
is at home.

KROGSTAD

I am afraid that is of no consequence to me.

NORA

What do you want?

KROGSTAD

I've been dismissed. I've been thrown out.

NORA

I'm terribly sorry but there was nothing I could do
about it. I tried everything but it wasn't any good.

KROGSTAD

You mean he cares so little about you that he'll ...

NORA

I haven't told him. He doesn't know!

KROGSTAD

I thought not. I don't see the noble Torvald risking
himself.

NORA

Mr Krogstad, you will speak of my husband with
respect in this house or not at all.

KROGSTAD

I know how much respect your beloved husband is
worth. (*He regards her shrewdly with an appraising
look.*) Still, I expect you've been giving the matter a
good deal of thought.

NORA

What do you want?

KROGSTAD

Your help. My livelihood has just been taken from me.

NORA

How can I help?

KROGSTAD

I don't think you understand the implications of what
you did.

NORA

Oh, I understand. (*She starts to cry.*)

KROGSTAD

There's no need to start getting upset. I know what
you're going through. As a matter of fact, you've
been on my mind all day. I expect that surprises you,
coming from a mere debt collector. My feelings, of
course, don't enter into it. What does it matter what
happens to me? How I'm treated. Oh, you can stop

looking like that. I'm not going to do anything. Not for the moment, anyway.

**NORA**

Oh! No, of course not. I never thought you would.

**KROGSTAD**

We can work something out between the three of us.

**NORA**

But Torvald mustn't know!

**KROGSTAD**

How are you going to stop that? By paying off what you owe me, here and now? That won't help. I'm not parting with that document. You can offer what you like for it.

**NORA**

Please!

**KROGSTAD**

No, no, no. That stays with me. And don't start getting silly ideas about running off, or doing something stupid.

**NORA**

How did you know?

**KROGSTAD**

It's what we all think of when we're trapped. Only most of us don't have the courage. I didn't.

**NORA**

No, nor I.

**KROGSTAD**

Well that's just as well since I have the information in any case, to use when and where I please. So doing

something desperate will solve nothing for you.
Look … all that's going to happen is a little domestic
upset. You'll soon get over it, and things will be back
to normal. I've written a letter …

NORA

I've told you, he mustn't know about it!

KROGSTAD

… telling him, in the gentlest possible way.

NORA

No, please, you must tear it up, please! I'll get the
money somehow.

KROGSTAD

I thought I'd made it clear to you …

NORA

I don't mean the money I owe you. Just tell me how
much more you want.

KROGSTAD

The money is not important! Can't I get that through
your head? I've been an outcast long enough! My
children are growing up – becoming aware. I am not
prepared to go on eating dirt – not any longer. I will
not be thrown down, not a second time.

NORA

I have asked him to let you stay!

KROGSTAD

That's not good enough. I've been giving the matter a
great deal of thought and it's become very clear to me.
You must inform your husband that I require instant
reinstatement at the bank … not in my former
position but in a new post that he will create for me. It

will then be seen that I withdrew in order to take on
more senior duties.

NORA

But he'd never do that!

KROGSTAD

I think he would. I think he would. You forget, I know
Torvald. He won't risk a scandal.

He paces up and down.

KROGSTAD

All I need is the opportunity. I know the running of
the bank far better than he does. Within a year, he
won't move without my advice. Ohh, you'll see, little
Mrs Helmer! It'll be Nils Krogstad in charge not
Torvald Helmer.

NORA

No, you won't.

KROGSTAD

Why not?

NORA

Because I won't let that happen. Whatever the cost.

KROGSTAD

Hah! Found the courage, have you?

NORA

Yes. Yes, I have. If necessary.

KROGSTAD

Don't try to frighten me.

NORA

Nor you me. If I have to, I shall do it.

KROGSTAD

I see. It's to be into the water, under the black ice, is it? Floating up next spring with your face swollen and ugly, your hair rotted away ...

NORA

You can't frighten me.

KROGSTAD

Nor you me. People don't do it, Mrs Helmer. They think about it but ... In any case, what good would it do? I have the document. Either your husband agrees to my proposal, or he's revealed as party to a fraud – whether you are in your coffin or not. So I advise you not to be stupid. What you must do is persuade Torvald to be sensible. I am sure you can manage it. Tell him, when he's read the letter, that I expect to hear from him.

He turns and goes.

NORA

(*Her hopes rising*) But he hasn't left the letter! (*She looks out into the hall*) Oh! He's put it in the letter box. It's there!

MRS LINDE enters with the dress.

MRS LINDE

I think this will do. Shall we try it on?

NORA

(*Hoarsely*) Kristina ... come here ...

MRS LINDE

(*Throws the dress on the back of the sofa*) Nora! Whatever's the matter?

NORA

Come here.

She takes MRS LINDE out into the hall.

NORA

Look ... There! Can you see? The letter. You can see it
through the glass panel.

MRS LINDE

Yes, I see it. Why?

NORA

It's from Krogstad.

MRS LINDE

Nora! He was the one who lent you the money! It was
Nils Krogstad!

NORA

Yes. And he's told Torvald.

MRS LINDE

But why now? Never mind, perhaps it's all for the
best. He really should be told.

NORA

You don't understand. I forged a signature.

MRS LINDE

Oh Nora. Oh my dear!

NORA

Kristina, I want you to be my witness ...

MRS LINDE

Witness? To what?

NORA

If I were to break down, for example ...

MRS LINDE

What?

NORA

... or if anything else were to happen. If I wasn't here
anymore.

MRS LINDE

Nonsense, you mustn't talk like that.

NORA

Don't you see? Torvald will try to take the blame on
himself!

MRS LINDE

How can you possibly think of ...

NORA

I want you to bear witness that I'm perfectly sane.
That I knew what I was doing, and that I did it alone.
Torvald knew nothing about it.

MRS LINDE

Of course, but I simply don't understand!

NORA

Oh, my poor Kristina, how could you? You've never
known a real marriage. Whatever happens, he'll try
to protect me. He'll destroy himself for me and for the
children. Well, I'm not going to let him. I won't allow
it.

MRS LINDE

Nora, I shall go and see Nils Krogstad at once.

NORA

No, you mustn't! He's desperate. There's no knowing
what he might do if you were to upset him.

MRS LINDE

There was a time when Nils would have done
anything for me.

NORA

Krogstad? I didn't know.

MRS LINDE

Give me his address.

NORA

I don't know where he lives. Wait a moment, Anna
gave me his card. *(She takes it from her pocket.)* But
what about the letter? It's there, in the box!

HELMER knocks from within.

HELMER

Nora, what are you doing? Let us in!

NORA

*(Frightened)* What is it? What do you want?

HELMER

Oh, all right. Are you trying on the dress?

NORA

Yes! Yes, wait till you see it! ...

MRS LINDE

*(Looking at the card)* It's not far.

NORA

What's the use?

MRS LINDE

Who keeps the key to the letter box?

NORA

Torvald. It's the only one.

MRS LINDE

Then Nils must ask for his letter back. He must find
an excuse.

NORA

It'll be too late. Torvald will have opened it.

MRS LINDE

Stop him. Put him off. I shan't be long, I promise.

MRS LINDE goes.

NORA moves about, in a panic, then crosses and opens the study
door.

NORA

Torvald ...

HELMER

So, I'm to be allowed into my own room at last! Come
along, Rank, now for the transformation scene. Oh, I
thought you said she was dressing up for us!

RANK

I must have got the wrong idea.

NORA

Don't be so impertinent. You'll see me at the dance
tomorrow, and not before.

HELMER

Darling, you look tired. What's the matter?

NORA

Nothing, nothing.

HELMER

Have you been rehearsing?

NORA

No I haven't.

HELMER

Then you should have been.

NORA

I need you to help me. I'm so nervous. I keep thinking
of all those people. I can't do it if you don't help me. I
know! You must stop working and give me the whole
evening. Will you? Just for me? Just for tonight?

HELMER

Very well. Let me fetch my letters.

NORA

No!

HELMER

Why not?

NORA

There's nothing there, I've looked.

HELMER

I'll just make sure.

She leaps to the piano, crashes out the opening bars of the
tarantella.

HELMER

(*Laughs*) Tara … tarara!

NORA

Now! This minute! If you don't help me this minute I
won't dance tomorrow!

HELMER

Good heavens, what a state you're in!

NORA

I'm nervous! Let's rehearse, there's just time before dinner. Quick ... you can play for me.

HELMER

(*Laughs*) If it's what you want.

He sits at the piano.

NORA takes a tambourine from the box and drapes a shawl around her shoulders.

NORA

Come on ... play!

She dances. RANK watches her.

HELMER

Slower ... not so fast!

NORA

I can't help it!

HELMER

Gently ...

But she dances more and more wildly. He stops playing.

HELMER

What are you doing? You're getting it all wrong.

NORA

You see? I told you! Torvald, you must help me.

RANK

I'll play for her, shall I?

HELMER

Good, then I can concentrate on the steps.

RANK plays.

HELMER calls out instructions. But NORA dances even more wildly, and beautifully, her hair falling about her shoulders.

MRS LINDE enters. She is spellbound.

#### MRS LINDE

Wonderful ... wonderful!

#### HELMER

Stop it! Nora! What the devil do you think you're doing? You're doing much too much. Rank. Rank, stop playing.

The DOCTOR stops.

#### HELMER

What on earth are you up to? Do you want to make a complete spectacle of yourself? What are people going to think? (*Silence.*) She's going much too far. I mean, good heavens, you're not dancing for your life.

NORA drops the tambourine. Silence.

#### HELMER

I don't understand. You've forgotten everything I taught you.

#### NORA

I know.

#### HELMER

We're going to have to work very hard. I'm not having you make a fool of yourself.

#### NORA

You see? I told you. I'll need coaching till the very last minute.

HELMER

I can see that.

NORA

Good! Tonight, and tomorrow, you're not to think
of anyone but me. You're to do nothing else, not
even the ... the letters. I forbid you to go near that
letterbox.

HELMER

Ah. I see. You're still worrying about that wretched
fellow.

NORA

Not at all. I'd forgotten all about it.

HELMER

Nora! It's perfectly obvious from your face that
there's a letter from him lying in the box out there.
Well?

NORA

If there is, you're not to read it. I forbid you to read
it. Not until tomorrow. I don't want anything coming
between us until after the dance.

RANK

(*Quietly*) I should give in to her, old chap.

HELMER

Oh, very well. You shall have your own way. But only
until tomorrow, mind.

NORA

That's all I want.

ANNA appears at the door.

ACT TWO


ANNA

Dinner is served.

NORA

Anna ... we'll have the champagne!

ANNA

Certainly, Miss Nora.

ANNA goes.

HELMER

Oh! A special celebration!

NORA

We'll drink champagne till dawn! Anna. *(She calls)* Anna, put out the macaroons, will you? I want macaroons, hundreds of them!

ANNA

*(Offstage)* Very good, Miss Nora.

HELMER

Now, now, now. Don't get so excited. I can't have my little bird in a state like this.

NORA

Don't worry. I'll be good. You and Doctor Rank go in. I'll just get Kristina to help me with my hair.

RANK

*(To HELMER, as they go)* I wonder. She's not expecting another child, is she?

HELMER

No, no. She just gets excited. You know how they are.

HELMER and RANK exit.

NORA

Well?

MRS LINDE

He wasn't there. He'll be back tomorrow night.

NORA

I knew by your face!

MRS LINDE

I've left a message for him.

NORA

In a way, it's almost exciting. I'm perfectly safe …
I'm married! I'm protected! He'll manage it somehow.
Make a miracle happen. Make everything right.

MRS LINDE

I'm sorry, I don't understand.

NORA

Poor dear Kristina, how could you? You've never had
a real marriage. I have a loving husband, so I've no
need to worry. He will take care of it – of everything.

MRS LINDE

Yes, of course he will.

NORA

You go in. I'll be with you in a second.

MRS LINDE exits.

NORA

No. I can't. I won't let him. He is not going to destroy
himself because of me.

She looks at her watch.

**NORA**

Seven hours to midnight, then twenty-four hours to midnight tomorrow, and the end of the dance. Thirty-one hours left. Thirty-one hours of life.

**HELMER**

(*At the door*) Come on – Nora? Where's my little bird?

**NORA**

(*Runs to him fervently*) Here I am!

*Fade to black.*

ACT THREE

The lamps are lit and the hall door is open. The sound of MUSIC.

MRS LINDE sits at the table reading a book. She finds it difficult to concentrate. More than once she listens.

MRS LINDE

(*Looks at her watch*) Oh come on! There's not much
time!

A pause and then a sound, off. She jumps to her feet, crosses, and lets in KROGSTAD.

MRS LINDE

Come in, come in. There's no-one about.

KROGSTAD

I got your note. What's the matter?

MRS LINDE

I wanted to talk to you.

KROGSTAD

Here? Why?

MRS LINDE

I had nowhere else. I can't very well ask you up to my
room. Come in, we're all on our own, the Helmers are
upstairs at the dance.

KROGSTAD

Dancing are they?

MRS LINDE

Why not?

104

KROGSTAD

Why not indeed?

MRS LINDE

Nils, I must talk to you.

KROGSTAD

I wouldn't have thought we had anything to say to
each other.

MRS LINDE

On the contrary, there's a great deal to be said.

KROGSTAD

Oh really?

MRS LINDE

You never understood, you know.

KROGSTAD

What was there to understand? It's the oldest story
in the world, a woman turning down her lover when
someone better off comes along.

MRS LINDE

If you knew. Do you think I found it easy?

KROGSTAD

It's the truth, isn't it? Well, isn't it? I still have the
letter you wrote me. You wrote that letter!

MRS LINDE

I had to. Under the circumstances, I felt that the least
I could do was try to kill your feeling for me. Nils, at
the time there was no other choice but to do what I
did.

KROGSTAD

Marry money, you mean?

MRS LINDE

My mother was bedridden – we were penniless! The boys were still tiny ... I couldn't see a way forward! I had to put my own feelings to one side. We couldn't wait for you, Nils. You couldn't have supported us for years. There was no other solution.

KROGSTAD

It was wrong. How could you do it?

MRS LINDE

I've asked myself that so many times.

KROGSTAD

It was wrong!

MRS LINDE

Have we the right to throw away happiness? I don't know.

KROGSTAD

You have no idea what you did. When I lost you, I lost the ground from under my feet. Look at me, look at what I've become. I'm wrecked. I'm like a man in the water, hanging on to a spar.

MRS LINDE

What makes you think rescue so impossible?

KROGSTAD

I don't. In fact, I was well on the way until you turned up here again to strike a second time.

MRS LINDE

Nils, I only learned today that it's you I'm to replace at the Bank.

KROGSTAD

*(Slight pause)* Well, if you say so. I suppose they didn't tell you. Now you know I hope you'll at least have the grace to resign.

MRS LINDE

I don't think that will help.

KROGSTAD

It might.

MRS LINDE

I'm afraid life has taught me not to act without a great deal of thought. I've learned that from necessity.

KROGSTAD

And I've learned not to believe in fine speeches.

MRS LINDE

I quite agree. *(She sits)* You believe in what people do?

KROGSTAD

What do you want?

MRS LINDE

You said that you felt lost?

KROGSTAD

Oh yes. Everything's been smashed for me, for a very long time.

MRS LINDE

Perhaps you're not the only one.

KROGSTAD

You're not asking for sympathy, are you? You deserted me, remember?

MRS LINDE

Because it was the only option at the time. How
could I abandon my own family? You must see that.
(Pause) Nils ... if two people who are alone ... who
have no-one ... if it were possible for them to ... join
forces ...

KROGSTAD

What?

MRS LINDE

Why do you think I came back?

KROGSTAD

Are you trying to say it was to see me? I don't believe
that.

MRS LINDE

(Slight pause) All my life, for as long as I can
remember, I've worked. But now I'm on my own.
There's no-one to work for any more. Nils, I can't
stand it! I need someone! There have always been
people to look after. It's who I am. What I do. Please ...
(She rises and walks about.) I know this must be
surprising for you, after all this time, but we're still
young ... young enough to ...

KROGSTAD

Rubbish. You're just trying to go for yet another noble
sacrifice. You seem to be good at that.

MRS LINDE

Oh, come on. Have you ever known me to make a
romantic gesture? I'm much too practical. That's been
my trouble.

KROGSTAD

You can't really mean it?

MRS LINDE

I do. Most sincerely.

KROGSTAD

Well.

There is a pause.

KROGSTAD

No, no. In any case, a lot of things have happened
since ...

MRS LINDE

Yes, I know.

KROGSTAD

Then you know that I've lost my reputation?

MRS LINDE

Yes. And I took your point that some of it may have
been my fault. Couldn't we work together, to change
things?

KROGSTAD

Kristina, how can you talk like this? You can't have
thought about it. Do you know what you're saying?

MRS LINDE

Yes. I have, and I do.

KROGSTAD

I see. Yes, I can see it in your face. But you can't really
mean that you want me ... now? Placed as I am?

MRS LINDE

Your children need a mother. I need someone to take
care of. We need each other, you and I. I believe in you.
I know you. The real you. Nils, if we were together,
why, I don't think there's anything I couldn't face.

KROGSTAD

(*Takes her hands*) You mean it? You really mean it?

She nods.

KROGSTAD

(*He kisses her hands.*) I can't take it in. When I
saw you, in this room, two days ago ... Kristina ...
Kristina! (*He embraces her.*) I can't believe it. (*He
touches her hair.*) I could start to live again. Put
everything right. I'd forgotten what it was to feel ...

MRS LINDE

Sssh ... (*She listens*) It's the tarantella. The dance
must be nearly over. They'll be down soon.

KROGSTAD

Yes, I'd better go. (*He stops short.*) Oh. Look, there's
something you don't know. It's not going to work. I'm
sorry.

MRS LINDE

Is it about the Helmers? About Nora?

KROGSTAD

Yes. You know about it?

MRS LINDE

She told me.

KROGSTAD

And you still want me?

MRS LINDE

Nils, believe me. I know only too well how far one can
be driven by necessity.

KROGSTAD

If I could only undo it.

MRS LINDE

But you can. Of course you can.

KROGSTAD

Perhaps you're right. I noticed my letter in the box as
I came in. I wrote to Helmer telling him everything.
Obviously, I must get it back before. (*A thought
strikes him and he gives her a hard look.*) Just a
minute. (*He thrusts her down onto the sofa with a
rough push.*) Is this what it's all about? Getting your
friend out of a mess? Is this why you've been ... ? I
have to know. You might as well be straight about it.

MRS LINDE

Nils, please! I've already sold myself once for the sake
of others. Believe me, I am not going to do it a second
time. I care for you. You've always known that.

KROGSTAD

I shall ask for the letter back.

MRS LINDE

Ye-es ... I suppose that would be for the best.

KROGSTAD

It'll be simple enough. I'll wait until Helmer comes
down and tell him that it is about my dismissal. That I
wrote it in anger and that I would rather have it back.
He'll understand.

MRS LINDE

I don't know.

KROGSTAD

What do you mean?

MRS LINDE

I've been thinking about it. I'm not at all sure that it
wouldn't be better to leave things as they are.

KROGSTAD

I don't understand. Isn't that one of the reasons you
asked me here in the first place?

MRS LINDE

Yes. But the more I think about the extra-ordinary
goings-on in this house, the more I'm inclined to
think that it's time certain things came out. All
this deceit, and people not knowing and concealing
things. If she won't tell him then the letter must. It's
making for unhappiness. Time it was all cleared up.

KROGSTAD

Well, if you think that's wise.

MRS LINDE

Nils, how can they be truly happy until there is
absolute honesty between them?

KROGSTAD

You're probably right. Very well. If you feel it proper
to take the risk, I'll be guided by you. There is
something I can do however, to put matters right. I
shall go and see to it at once.

MRS LINDE

(Listens) Yes, I think perhaps you'd better go. That's
the end of the dance. They'll be down in a minute.

KROGSTAD

May I wait for you downstairs in the hall?

MRS LINDE

Oh please do! Then you can see me home!

KROGSTAD

Kristina ... (*He embraces her.*) I can't believe it! It's
the most amazing thing that's ever happened to me.
It's hard to believe, that one might actually be happy.
I'll wait for you.

KROGSTAD goes, leaving the inner doors open.

MRS LINDE

(*Begins to tidy*) What a difference it will make! (*She
puts on her hat, and readies her coat*) My own family!
Someone to work for – take care of. Oh, I can't wait to
make them comfortable, look after things ... not to
be alone anymore! Come on! Hurry up! (*She listens,
waiting to be released.*) Ah, here they are. (*She puts
on her coat.*)

HELMER and NORA are heard arguing.

HELMER almost forces NORA into the room. He is in evening dress,
she in costume.

NORA

No, Torvald, it's too early!

HELMER

Nora darling ...

NORA

Please, Torvald, just a little longer please ...

HELMER

Now, you know what I said. Come in, or you'll catch cold. (*He gently propels her inside.*)

MRS LINDE

Hullo ... good evening.

NORA

Oh ... Kristina ... !

HELMER

Hullo, Mrs Linde, what on earth are you doing up so late?

MRS LINDE

Forgive me. I so wanted to see Nora in her costume.

NORA

Have you been waiting long?

MRS LINDE

No, no. I couldn't get here before you went up.

NORA

I understand.

HELMER

Doesn't she look magnificent, Mrs Linde?

MRS LINDE

She certainly does.

HELMER

Enchanting! Everyone thought so. But what a stubborn girl! Do you know, do you know, I almost had to drag her away? I had the dickens of a job!

NORA

I only wanted a little longer. We could go back now.

HELMER

There ... do you see? Ah, but she danced the
tarantella beautifully. Perhaps just a little wilder
than was absolutely required for an artistic
performance but no ... no, they were all ecstatic about
her. Which was the moment to leave. If we'd stayed,
the whole effect would have been ruined. I wasn't
having that! I picked up my lovely Capri girl. I should
say my <u>capricious</u> Capri girl, ha ha ha! I whisked her
round the room, and away! The dream, as they say,
vanished! Very important to make the proper exit.
But can I get my little Nora to see that, Mrs Linde? ...
Ouf, I'm hot! Hang on, I'll get another lamp. We can't
see ourselves.

He throws his cloak over the sofa, and exits into the study

NORA

(*Urgent whisper*) Have you seen him?

MRS LINDE

Yes, I've talked to him.

NORA

Well?

MRS LINDE

Nora, you must tell your husband.

NORA

(*Dully*) I knew it.

MRS LINDE

No, you don't understand. There's nothing to fear
from Nils now. That's all been arranged. But this can't
go on. You must tell your husband.

NORA

No.

MRS LINDE

Nora, why be stubborn?

NORA

No!

MRS LINDE

Then I'm afraid the letter will.

NORA

Never mind, Kristina. Thank you anyway. No, no, it doesn't matter. Thank you for trying. It's all right. I know what I must do.

MRS LINDE

Now be sensible, won't you?

HELMER

(Enters) Still here, Mrs Linde?

MRS LINDE

Yes indeed. And now I must go.

HELMER

Oh, already?

MRS LINDE

Goodnight, Nora. Now you won't be stubborn, will you? It's all for the best, believe me.

HELMER

That's what I keep telling her!

MRS LINDE

Goodnight, Mr Helmer. Goodnight.

HELMER

*(Sees her to the door.)* Goodnight ... perhaps I should? ... but you're just around the corner, aren't you?

MRS LINDE

No, no, you mustn't think of it.

HELMER

Goodnight. *(He closes the door.)* My God what a boring woman. I thought she'd never go.

NORA

Are you tired?

HELMER

No, wide awake, very lively! What about my girl?

NORA

Oh, I could drop off any minute.

HELMER

There, I was right, wasn't I? To leave when we did?

NORA

Yes.

HELMER

That's more like it. *(Fondling her)* The doctor was cheerful tonight – did you notice?

NORA

I wasn't looking.

HELMER

He hasn't been in such spirits for ages. Oh, it's so good to be alone ... my lovely girl. Shall I tell you something? I've been wanting you all evening. Why do you think I dragged you away? I've been playing

a little game, pretending that we're secret lovers.
Sometimes I pretend you're my new young bride and
I'm going to discover you for the first time . . .

NORA

Torvald no . . . don't. Not now. I don't want to.

HELMER

What do you mean, you don't want to? You can't say
that. I'm your husband . . .

A KNOCK at the door.

NORA

(Jumps) Listen!

HELMER

Who's that?

RANK

(Outside) It's only me. May I come in for a moment?

HELMER

(Irritable) What the devil does he want? (At the door)
My dear fellow, good of you to drop in on your way
down.

RANK

I heard you talking, I hope you don't mind.

NORA and HELMER regard him without speaking as he strolls
about the room.

RANK

This dear place. How I've enjoyed being here with
you. I so love this room.

HELMER

You seemed to be having a pretty good time upstairs.

RANK

Why not, while you can? The wine was very good I
thought.

HELMER

Yes, excellent champagne.

RANK

I managed to put away an amazing amount.

NORA

Torvald's drunk.

RANK

You too?

NORA

Champagne always makes him ... cheerful.

RANK

And why not?

HELMER

Why not indeed?

A pause. HELMER moves away.

NORA

(To RANK) You're in a splendid mood. Oh, have you
heard the results of your tests?

HELMER

What?

NORA

The doctor was making some tests. In his laboratory.

HELMER

Laboratory, what do you know about laboratories?

NORA

(*To RANK*) Was there a result? Am I to congratulate you?

RANK

Yes. Yes, I think you may.

NORA

A good result?

RANK

You might put it that way. At all events, a certainty.

NORA

A certainty?

RANK

Yes. So, an evening of celebration was in order, don't you agree?

NORA

Oh Doctor, I think you're fond of masquerades.

HELMER

Hah, what are you doing, planning next year's dance? What shall she go as, Rank?

RANK

She must go as the spirit of light ... of happiness!

HELMER

Sounds a funny idea. What can you wear for that?

RANK

Oh, I would say that if she just wore her everyday things, that would be perfectly in character.

NORA takes the DOCTOR's hand impulsively.

HELMER

Very nicely put. Very nicely put. And what about you?

RANK

Me? Ah. I shall be invisible.

HELMER

Funny sort of costume.

RANK

Haven't you heard of the cloak of invisibility? You put it on and no-one can see you.

HELMER

(*Suppressing a grin*) Well if you say so, old chap. I'm sure you're right. Very good idea.

Hiatus. No-one speaks. RANK realises they may want him to go.

RANK

Oh, I forgot what I came for. May I have one of your Havanas?

HELMER

Certainly, my dear fellow. With my compliments.

RANK

(*Cuts the end of the cigar*) Thank you.

NORA

(*Strikes a match for him*) Let me light it for you.

RANK

Thank you. (*He lights his cigar.*) And now I must bid you goodbye.

HELMER

Goodnight, my dear chap.

NORA

I hope you have a good night.

RANK

My thanks for the thought.

NORA

And will you wish me the same?

RANK

My dear, do you need it? Very well, by all means.
Sleep well. And thank you for the light.

He stands for a moment, then nods to them abruptly and goes.

HELMER

(*Murmurs*) He's drunk.

NORA

(*Absently*) I daresay.

HELMER takes out his keys, and exits into the hall.

NORA

Torvald what are you doing?

HELMER

(*Offstage*) Emptying the letterbox. There won't be
room for the papers if I don't. Hullo, someone's been at
the lock! Come and look.

NORA goes out into the hall.

HELMER

(*Off*) It can't have been one of the maids, can it?

NORA

(*Off– quickly*) It must have been the children.

HELMER

(*Off*) Put a stop to it. We can't have this sort of behaviour. Ah that's it, I've done it! Anna, put out the light on the landing, will you? Hullo, what's this?

NORA

(*Off. Murmurs sadly*) No ...

HELMER

(*Off*) Rank's left a visiting card. What do you make of that?

NORA

(*Off*) Let me see.

HELMER

(*Off*) He's drawn a cross by his name. Rather sinister, don't you think? Almost as if he were announcing his own death.

NORA

(*Off*) He is.

NORA enters, followed by HELMER

HELMER

What do you mean? Has he said anything?

NORA

It's his way of saying goodbye to us. He's going to shut himself up on his own to die.

HELMER

Ugh! Poor old Rank. I'd no idea. I mean, I knew he hadn't long, but so soon ... and to go off like that, like a wounded animal ...

NORA

Isn't it best, to go off without a word? Isn't that best, Torvald?

HELMER

I can't imagine being without him. He's such a part of our life. His dark, funny ways. His depressions. Somehow, he's always been the cloud to our sunshine. The background to our happiness. I suppose it's all for the best. We shall be on our own now, just the two of us. Yes, perhaps it's all for the best. *(He puts his arms around her.)* Oh, my love, I can never hold you enough. I've even dreamed of terrible dangers threatening you, just so that I could rescue you, risk my life to save yours.

NORA

*(Frees herself, and speaks clearly and calmly)* Torvald. Torvald, you must read your letters now.

HELMER

No, no ... not now. I want to be with my lovely wife ...

NORA

Even when your best friend is dying?

HELMER

Oh ... yes. You're right of course. It wouldn't be the thing. Anyway, it's made a funny atmosphere, all this talk of death. I hate that sort of thing. We won't tonight, darling. Plenty of time for us.

NORA

*(Puts her arms round his neck and kisses him.)* Goodnight, Torvald. Goodnight, my love ... goodnight!

HELMER

(*Kisses her*) I'll just read my letters.

He goes into the study with the letters.

NORA, wide-eyed with shock, moves about the room.

She picks up HELMER's cloak and throws it about her shoulders.

NORA

(*Whispers to herself*) I shan't ever see him again.
Never see the children. Oh God, please give me
strength. If only it were over. (*She pulls a shawl over
her head.*) Oh, my loves, goodbye ... I love you ...

She kisses their pictures and turns to go.

TORVALD throws open the study door, the letter in his hand.

HELMER

Nora!

She screams with fright.

HELMER

What is this?! Do you know what this letter says?

She makes for the door but he cuts her off.

NORA

Let me go! (*He blocks her path.*) Let me go!

HELMER

Go? Go where?

NORA

(*Struggling*) Let me go. You are not going to sacrifice
yourself for me. I won't have it!

HELMER

Stop it. Stop being hysterical. You mean it's true? Is
this the truth? No, it can't be. I don't believe it. It's
impossible. My wife, a common criminal?

NORA

I've loved you more than anything in the world . . .

HELMER

Look, I don't want your silly excuses.

NORA

It was for you!

HELMER

And you can stop being hysterical. (*He locks the
door.*) Right. Now you will stay here until I get a full
account of all this. Do you realise what you have
done? Well answer me, do you?

NORA

Yes.

HELMER

My God, I can't take it in! You've been my proudest
possession! When I think of it! The lies! The deceit!
All these years when I've believed you to be . . . Of
course, I should have known. I should have seen
it. You're like your father. All that charm, and the
shadiness with it. No proper sense of responsibility.
And this is what I get for helping him . . . which I did
for your sake! I condoned recklessness, for you! Well,
this is how I'm repaid for it.

NORA

Yes.

HELMER

You realise you've ruined me. You've destroyed my
future. It doesn't bear thinking of! I'm in the hands . . .
I'm totally in the hands of a dishonest rogue who can
do just as he wants with me.

NORA

Not when I'm out of the way. You'll be free then.

HELMER

Out of the way? What do you mean? Whether you're
here or not will make no difference. People will still
think I put you up to it. Your running off isn't going
to solve anything, so you can put that out of your
mind. When I think of it! You've had my total love
and protection, and this is how you repay me. By
destroying my career. You realise what you've done?

NORA

Yes.

HELMER

I can't take it in. There must be some way out. Take
that coat off. Take it off, I say! I shall have to get
round the man. Persuade him somehow. It'll all have
to be hushed up, God knows at what price! Ugh. As
for you and me, well, that's another matter. As far as
other people are concerned, we shall have to carry on
as though nothing's happened. You will remain here,
under my roof, but only under strict conditions. The
children must be removed from you for a start. Oh!
To think of saying this to someone I . . . someone I still
find . . . (*He almost breaks down.*) But no, that's over.
It will simply be a question of picking up the pieces
from now on. Maintaining a decent facade.

The doorbell rings. He jumps, alarmed.

HELMER

Who the devil is that? Oh, my God, you don't think
it's . . . ? Look, you'd better hide in there. Quick, keep
out of sight!

But NORA does not move.

ANNA comes to the door in her night clothes.

ANNA

There's a letter for you, Miss Nora.

NORA

Thank you.

HELMER

Give it to me.

He snatches the letter from ANNA, closes the door after her, and
rips open the envelope.

HELMER

Yes! It's from Krogstad! No, you are not to touch it! I
shall read it myself!

NORA

Very well.

HELMER

(*Goes to the lamp.*) I can hardly bear to. He's probably
finished me. (*He groans, reads a few lines, looks at
the enclosed document in disbelief and then shouts
with relief.*) Nora . . . Nora! No wait, I must read it
again! It's all right. It's all right . . . I'm saved! I'm
saved, Nora, I'm saved!

NORA

What about me?

HELMER

You too, of course, my darling! It's over! We're saved!
Look, he's sent back your bond. He says that he's
deeply sorry. That he bitterly regrets what he felt
forced to do. That something has happened in his life
that's changed everything! Oh, never mind all this.
What does it matter? We're saved! With this in my
hand, there is no proof against you! I'll destroy the
damned thing at once. I don't even want to look at
it. (*He rips up the bond and throws it on the stove.*)
There! All gone! My poor girl. (*Glancing at the letter.*)
He says you've known all over Christmas. You must
have been out of your mind with worry!

NORA

Yes.

HELMER

Oh my love! And to think that ... I mean, that you
even thought of going! No! We won't dwell on it. We'll
forget the whole nasty business. It's over. Done with.
(*He glances at her.*) What's the matter? Why such a
long face? Can't you take it in? My poor little Nora. I
know what's the matter. You're thinking ... Look, I'm
not going to hold it against you. I forgive you. I forgive
you, Nora! It's true that you did go behind my back.
And you did lie to me. What you did was very, very
irregular. But it <u>was</u> done for me.

NORA

Yes. It was.

HELMER

How could you possibly realise the risk you were
taking? That what you were doing was wrong? You
loved me as a wife should love her husband. It was
just your lack of experience. You didn't understand
the significance of what you were doing. Believe me, I
don't love you any the less because you can't manage
these things. It's not in your nature. It's part of your
attraction for me. Nonetheless, you must learn to
rely – to lean on me. That's what I'm here for. To take
care of you all. Now you must forget the harsh things
I said just now. I was upset. After all, it did seem as
though you'd brought my whole life and career down
about my ears – and what would have become of us all
then … eh? The main thing is I've forgiven you. We'll
forget all about it.

NORA

(*Quietly*) Thank you. For the forgiveness.

She crosses to the nursery door and exits.

HELMER

Where are you going?

NORA

(*Offstage*) I'm taking off my costume.

HELMER

Good. Yes. Do that. Time for bed. My poor little bird,
you looked so crushed. All over now. You can calm
down. Just remember, my wings are big enough for
both of us. (*He sits, relaxing on the sofa.*) What a dear,
secure place this is! It's where you belong – where I
can protect my little dove in her nest. Now you're to
stop worrying. We'll go to bed and, in the morning,

everything will be forgotten. Oh Nora, it's such a warm, generous feeling – this feeling of forgiveness. When a man forgives a woman, it makes her doubly his. She is his wife and, at the same time, his child – to be guided by him. You're safe, my love. But promise me one thing. That you will never, ever deceive me again. Just be open with me. Let me be your conscience. Hullo? What's this? I thought you were getting ready for bed.

NORA appears in her day clothes.

NORA

I changed.

HELMER

What for?

NORA

Sit down, Torvald. You and I have a lot to say to each other. (*She sits across the table from him.*) I think you'd better sit down.

HELMER

(*Sits opposite her*) Nora, don't frighten me like this. What's the matter with you? I don't understand you.

NORA

No, you don't understand me. And I've never understood you. Until tonight, that is. No. Please don't interrupt. I'd rather you listened. It's time we faced facts, Torvald.

HELMER

What's that supposed to mean?

NORA

(*Slight pause*) Doesn't it strike you as odd, the way we're both sitting here together?

HELMER

No, why should it?

NORA

We've been married for eight years, and this is the first time we've ever sat down together for a serious discussion.

HELMER

How do you mean, serious?

NORA

In eight years, we've never exchanged a serious word, on anything at all.

HELMER

But why should I bother you with all my problems? It's not as though they're matters you could help me with.

NORA

I wasn't actually thinking of your affairs.

HELMER

But Nora, dearest. What would be the point?

NORA

That is my point. You've never understood the first thing about me. I've been cheated. First by my father, and then by you.

HELMER

What on earth are you talking about? Your father
and I? The two people who've loved you more than
anything in the world?

NORA

Torvald, you've never loved me.

HELMER

(*Very shocked*) What do you mean?!

NORA

You've merely found it extremely pleasant to be in
love with me.

HELMER

Nonsense!

NORA

It's true. When I lived at home, the only opinions
allowed were Papa's. What he thought, we thought.
Believe me, we kept very quiet otherwise. It wouldn't
have done to disagree. He used to call me his little
doll. He liked to play with me just as I played with my
own dolls in the nursery. Then, when I came here, to
your house ...

HELMER

<u>My</u> house? Is that how you think of our home?

NORA

(*Unshaken*) I mean, when I was handed over from
Papa to you. From his hands to yours. It's <u>your</u> house.
Everything here is arranged to suit you. Everything
is to your taste. I simply follow you instead of Papa.
What you like, I like. Well, sometimes there's a little
of both of us. It's hard to say all the time. But when I

think about it, I've lived here just as I did with Papa. On sufferance, like a beggar. I've done tricks for you. Performed – in exchange for my bed and board. That's been the arrangement. Your arrangement. Yours and Papa's. I've done nothing with my life, because you've cheated me out of it. Both of you. I've been cheated.

HELMER

Nora, that's being totally unreasonable. And, I may say, ungrateful. Don't I look after you? Haven't you been happy here?

NORA

No. Never. I thought I was, but I realise now. No. I've never been happy here. Merely high-spirited. I've been cheerful. To please you. I'm not saying you've been unkind, Torvald. You've always been extremely kind to me. But this house is a playroom. You play with me, just as Papa did. You treat me like a toy. Something to amuse you. Something to play with. Just as I play with the children. I treat my own children in just the same way. It's not surprising. That's what our marriage has been, Torvald. A playroom.

HELMER

(After a pause) There may be something in what you say. I think you overstate the case. All right, from now on, things can be different. A new beginning. Playtime is over. Time for lessons now.

NORA

Not from you, Torvald. You can't teach me.

HELMER

Why not?

NORA

I need to know how to fit myself to rear our children.
You said yourself, just now – that you didn't dare
trust them to me.

HELMER

That was in the heat of the moment. I was upset.
Surely you didn't take me seriously?

NORA

But you were absolutely right. I'm not at all fitted
for it. How can I possibly influence my children –
see to their care, their education – when I'm totally
untrained? I need to educate myself. It's not
something you can do for me. *(Slight pause)* Which is
why I'm leaving you.

HELMER

What? What are you talking about?

NORA

If I am to understand myself and the world around me
I must first learn to stand on my own two feet. That is
why I cannot stay here any longer.

HELMER

Nora!

NORA

I'm going now, at once. Kristina can give me a bed for
the night.

HELMER

You're mad. You're out of your mind! I forbid it!

NORA

I'm afraid it's useless for you to forbid me anything anymore. I shall take only the things that belong to me. I don't want anything from you – now or ever.

HELMER

Have you gone completely out of your mind?

NORA

I'm going home tomorrow. Back where I came from. It'll be easier for me to find something to do there.

HELMER

How can you be so silly? So blind? Everything you say shows your total lack of experience!

NORA

Then it's high time I acquired some.

HELMER

But to leave your home, your husband . . . your children. What are people going to say?

NORA

I can't allow that to influence me. I only know what I must do.

HELMER

It's outrageous! How can you – a woman – turn your back on your most sacred commitments?

NORA

And what do you consider those to be?

HELMER

Do I have to remind you? Your responsibility to your husband and your children.

NORA

I consider that I have another duty, equally sacred.

HELMER

Nonsense. What?

NORA

My duty to myself.

HELMER

But you are first and foremost a wife and a mother!

NORA

I don't believe that any more. I believe that I am,
first and foremost, a human being, like yourself. At
any rate, I shall try to become one. Oh, I'm sure most
people will agree with you. I'm sure all the books
say so. Frankly, I'm not interested in being told who
and what I am any longer. I'm no longer interested in
trying to fulfil all the roles and purposes created for
me by others. I need to discover my own life, to find
out for myself. I have a lot of thinking to do. I want my
own answers.

HELMER

But you can find those here. Where you belong. In
your own home! And you've no need to look further
than your religion. You'll find all the answers there if
you take the trouble to look.

NORA

Torvald, I don't know what religion is.

HELMER

What!

NORA

All I know is what I was taught by Pastor Hansen.
When I get away from here, and can think and read
for myself, I'm going to investigate. I shall see if what
he taught me was true. Or, more particularly, if it is
true for me.

HELMER

It's unthinkable! A young woman like you can't talk
like this! If you won't be guided by religion, at least
listen to your own conscience. I presume you have
some moral feelings somewhere?

NORA

Oh Torvald, how do I know? I can't answer you. I have
no answers. I only know that things are not at all as
I supposed them to be. And that I think very, very
differently from you. I find that the law is not what I
understood it to be. And, however much I think about
it, I cannot see that the law is in the right. A law that
prevents a woman from sparing her father on his
deathbed – which prevents her from trying to save
the life of her own husband … If matters are, indeed,
so organised, then it is wrong. I can't agree to it.

HELMER

You're talking like a child. You have no idea how
society functions.

NORA

I agree. That is why I must go and find out. I need to
learn, and discover, and understand. Then I shall be
able to see who is in the right … society or me.

ACT THREE

HELMER

Nora, I think you must be ill. You've probably got a
fever. Yes, that's what it is. You're not talking sense.

NORA

I've never been more clear-headed in my life.

HELMER

So clear-headed that you can sit there, calmly
announcing that you are about to abandon your own
husband and children!

NORA

Yes.

A pause.

HELMER

(*Low*) Then there's only one possible explanation.

NORA

What do you mean?

HELMER

You don't love me anymore.

NORA

Exactly.

HELMER

Nora! How can you talk like this? How can you say
such things!

NORA

I know. It's very hard for me, Torvald. You've always
been very kind to me. But I can't help it. I don't love
you anymore.

HELMER

(*Controlling his voice with difficulty*) Are you are
clear- headed about that too?

NORA

Yes. Yes. That's why I can't go on living here with you.

HELMER

(*Slight pause*) Perhaps you could explain why. Why
I've come to lose your love?

NORA

It was this evening. I expected a miracle. I had no
doubt about it. No doubt at all. I was disappointed. You
are not the man I believed you to be.

HELMER

I don't understand. What do you mean?

NORA

I'd looked for it, for eight years. I've been waiting –
oh, not impatiently. God knows, I didn't seek the
occasion. But I knew it would come, one day. One day
I would have the proof I needed ... an indication ... an
action performed that would be an explanation ... the
justification for my life.

HELMER

What are you talking about?

NORA

As I say, you don't look for crisis. But when this
awful thing happened I thought, yes! Yes, this is it!
I'll get my proof! I'll know, for sure. You see, it never
occurred to me – not for one moment – that you would
allow him to threaten me. That you would succumb
to blackmail. That you would submit. I was convinced

that you would simply say to him: 'Go away. Publish
what you want. 'Tell the world!' It simply never
occurred to me that you would not be my champion.

HELMER

I see. You allowed yourself to believe that I would
disgrace myself for your dishonesty?

NORA

I was absolutely certain of it. More than that. I was
convinced . . . I assumed you would insist on taking
the blame yourself. That you would pretend that the
fraud had been your idea.

HELMER

Nora!

NORA

I hope you know me well enough to know that I
wouldn't . . . I couldn't let you make such a sacrifice.
But I assumed that you would try. I assumed that you
would defend me, as Daddy did. As you have always
said it was your loving duty and responsibility to do.
This was my dilemma. How could I save you from the
consequences of your own gallantry? From the role
in which you have undoubtedly always seen yourself.
Which you have displayed to me – and on which our
whole relationship is based? The role of your care
and domination. I could see only one way to rescue
you from the mess I found myself in, and which
threatened you too. I would have to take my life.

Slight pause.

HELMER

Nora, please, you must understand. I'm prepared to
work all my life for you. Day and night. I'll endure any
hardship for your sake. But a man can't sacrifice his
honour, not even for the woman he loves.

NORA

Women do. All the time.

HELMER

That's romantic nonsense.

NORA

Perhaps. But I've been misled. Nothing is as I thought.
There is something wrong with the rules. You are not
the person I believed you to be.

HELMER

Look, if . . .

NORA

When you read that letter, you went into a blind
panic. Did you once think of the misery I'd endured
all those years? For you, for your sake? Why do you
think I borrowed the money in the first place? Must
I remind you that it was for you? The doctors told
me that your lungs were going. That you might die.
That the one chance of saving you was to take you
to the sun. And I did it! If Papa had not been so ill,
he would have signed the bond for me. I was only
fulfilling what I knew would have been his wish too.
To save your life! Did you pause to think? Did you
dwell on any of this? You had only one thought. Your
reputation. Your standing among other men – your
colleagues, your rivals. When, and only when, you
realised that the danger was over. Then, and only

then, did you graciously condescend to 'forgive' me. What sort of morality are we talking about? I have been misled! The moment you thought we were safe, then I must be the doll, the plaything, again. Oh, a bit more tissue paper, perhaps, to shelter me. Shelter me from what? From whom? For eight years, I have been living with a stranger. With a man I neither know nor want to know. I've had three children by you! The thought destroys me! I could tear my womb out thinking about it!

A pause.

> HELMER
>
> (*Sadly*) Yes. Yes, I see. I see. I do see. There's a huge gulf opened up between us. But Nora, couldn't we bridge it somehow?

> NORA
>
> I've changed. I don't know if I'm the wife for you now.

> HELMER
>
> But to lose you, Nora. I can't ... I can't bear it! I just can't imagine this happening.

NORA exits into the hall.

She returns with her coat and a small bag. She puts on her hat and coat.

> HELMER
>
> No, please. Not now. Nora ... look ... wait till morning.

> NORA
>
> How can I spend the night in the house of a man I don't know?

HELMER

We could sleep apart.

NORA

(*Fastening her hat*) Torvald, you know how long that
would last. Goodbye. I'm not going to see the children.
They're in far better hands than mine. As I am now,
I'm not in the least fitted to look after them.

HELMER

But soon, Nora. Later on. Sometime ...

NORA

How can I say?

HELMER

You're still my wife.

NORA

I'm setting you free. Here. Your ring. You'd better give
me mine.

A pause.

HELMER

Very well. (*He takes off his ring.*)

NORA

Thank you. Here are the keys. There won't be any
trouble. The servants know far more about running
the house than I've ever done. I'll ask Kristina to call
for my things. She can send them on to me.

HELMER

Is this it, then? You're going to forget me?

NORA

Of course not. I shall think of you often. This house ...
the children ...

HELMER

May I write to you?

NORA

No.

HELMER

Can't I help you if you need it? At least let me ...

NORA

How can I possibly accept help from a stranger?

HELMER

Do you really mean that I can never, ever be more
than that to you?

NORA

(*Picking up her bag*) Torvald, there would have to be
the most amazing miracle ...

HELMER

But what ... how? Tell me how.

NORA

We would <u>both</u> have to change. I'm sorry. I don't
believe in miracles anymore.

HELMER

But I do. I will. How do you mean, we must both
change. How?

NORA

In such a way – so completely – that there could be a
real marriage between us. (*Slight pause.*) Goodbye.

NORA goes.

HELMER sinks into his chair and buries his face in his hands.

HELMER

Nora . . . Nora . . . (*He lifts his head. in disbelief*)

She's gone!

Below, the door to the street clangs shut.

*Fade to black.*

The End

# GHOSTS

by Henrik Ibsen

in a version by Pam Gems

Literal translation from the Norwegian
by Charlotte Barslund

for Sean Mathias

This version of Ghosts was produced by the SHERMAN
THEATRE COMPANY in Cardiff, Wales, in 1993, with the following cast:

| | |
|---|---|
| Regine | LISA PALFREY |
| Engstrand | DORIEN THOMAS |
| Pastor Manders | JOHN QUENTIN |
| Mrs Alving | SIAN PHILLIPS |
| Osvald | BRENDAN O'HEA |
| Directed by | SEAN MATHIAS |

# GHOSTS

Ibsen wrote GHOSTS in 1881, two years after A DOLL'S HOUSE. He said: "Ghosts had to be written. I could not let *A Doll's House* be my last word. After Nora, Mrs Alving had to come."

Ibsen was well aware that writing a play about sexual disease would create a storm. It did.

'One of the filthiest things ever written; a repulsive patho-logical phenomenon which, by undermining the morality of our social order, threatens its foundation.'

(Royal Theatre, Copenhagen.)

'An open drain; a loathsome sore unbandaged; a dirty act, loathsome and fetid.'

(Press reaction to London production in 1891.)

And so, the play has remained, ever since, as the shock-ing drama that took the lid off sexual disease.

Nonetheless, Ibsen's stature grew. He became known as the First Modern Writer. He was serious. When you consider his themes: – the emancipation of women, dirty politics, the corrosions of greed and personal ambition – these are themes for a giant.

Henrik Ibsen can easily seem to be a chilly God, up there on Parnassus, where the oxygen is thin and the air bites the nose.

Respect, yes. But respect in theatre is deadly.

How does one approach a classic? You look for the truth, and mine out what has pierced the imagination. And the first, general, blazing truth about Ibsen is that, unlike the detached Dr Chekhov with his sly scalpel, Ibsen is not cool at all. He is white-hot. There is nothing of the aloof Thomas Mann about him, and nothing of the academician, thank God.

Ibsen rages with feeling. Like Santiago in Hemingway's

The Old Man and the Sea, he fishes with a long line, and hauls up strange denizens of the deep. A dramatist who writes about sexual disease in Norway in 1881 is very courageous. His reward was to be acclaimed, ultimately, for his social commitment.

The irony is, that this isn't the play at all. We are led to believe that GHOSTS is about a woman desecrated and infected by a libidinous husband, and passing on the disease to her beloved child. But that's only part of it. Mrs Alving's voyage of discovery is even more shocking. The play, we discover, is about passion, about lust for life – sexual life – and the deadly consequences of its denial. Yet how can it be possible (given the tragic consequences of inherited syphilis in the tertiary stage), not to condemn licence?

Ibsen's portrayal of Hélène Alving, one of the great female roles in the theatrical canon, is breath-taking in its daring. It is she, rather than Nora in A DOLL'S HOUSE, who is the proto-feminist. It is Mrs Alving who becomes aware that she is not a victim (the fatal aberration of much neo-feminism) but a protagonist.

An adult human being is not a helpless pawn of sex or social circumstances, but a creature capable of, and impelled to make, choices. She understands, too late, the inadequacy of remaining in the unquestioning obedience of the child-state.

At the end of the play – in pain for Osvald's terrible destiny – we see that his father is to blame and not to blame. Mrs Alving realizes that her youthful imprinting has been, at best, inadequate, making her a dutiful and dreary non-wife, denying herself as well as her husband full and joyous union, and driving him to solace and relief elsewhere.

For a play that is tragic in essence, there is a lot of humour (not always seen in production.) The minor characters are portrayed with wonderful mischief. Regine, Osvald's illegitimate half-sister, is a bitch – a Becky Sharp. She is, as Osvald observes wistfully, a survivor. Uninfected, she survives by sagacity and a hard heart. Of all the people in the play, she is the realist.

Jakob Engstrand, her putative father, is an outrageous rogue. A liar, drunkard, and a manipulative sponger. His arias of benevolent righteousness, as he effortlessly gulls Paster Manders, are glorious to watch.

The Pastor himself is a lethal tilt at the self-delusory power of the cloth. Manders is not a bad man. Nonetheless, he creates moral mayhem wherever he treads. He is a walking miasma of received beliefs, with deadly feelers of interference in the lives of others. Mrs Alving (who loves him) does not judge him for being a gullible fool. But she *does* judge him for destroying both their lives by his earlier unwillingness to face truth – in particular, sexual truth. Denying truth means you die, or go bad inside.

Ibsen's characters are like us. Unpredictable. They don't obey their own rules. They surprise themselves, and us. They get in a mess, like we do. They survive at a price, like we do. They are envious, heroic, frightened, amusing, despicable, shrewd, and wilful – like we are. And, like us, his protagonists are faced with sexual dilemmas.

Those dilemmas have changed radically in these existential times of chemical mutation and the side-lining of fecundity, which give too many choices in place of too few.

But Ibsen's theme is as potent as ever. Grow up, the play says, or go to the devil. His piercing humanity is not Tolstoy's. It does not spill over in our laps. But it is there. Heart-breaking, and enough to melt mountains.

Pam Gems 1993

# GHOSTS

## CAST

| | |
|---|---|
| MRS HELENE ALVING | Captain Alving's widow. |
| OSVALD ALVING | her son, a painter. |
| PASTOR MANDERS | |
| ENGSTRAND | a carpenter |
| REGINE ENGSTRAND | in Mrs Alving's service. |

The action takes place on Mrs Alving's country estate by a large fjord in Western Norway.

# GHOSTS

## ACT ONE

### ACT ONE – SCENE ONE

A large room, informal, with a round table, chairs, magazines and books on the table. A conservatory beyond, leading to the garden. The fjord can be glimpsed through the rain.

ENGSTRAND is at the door into the conservatory. He is crippled and wears a surgical boot. REGINE is trying to stop him from coming in.

> REGINE
>
> No, you can't. Stay there, you're dripping wet!

> ENGSTRAND
>
> It's only rain. God's rain.

> REGINE
>
> The devil's rain, you mean.

> ENGSTRAND
>
> Your tongue, Regine. *(He dodges round her.)*

> REGINE
>
> No!

> ENGSTRAND
>
> *(Evades her and comes in.)* I want to talk to you.

> REGINE
>
> Sssh! And stop banging about with that foot. The young master's trying to sleep.

ENGSTRAND

Sleep? At this time of day?

REGINE

What if he is? It's none of your business.

ENGSTRAND

Listen, I was out having a drink last night …

REGINE

Ooh, what a surprise.

ENGSTRAND

We're all human. Some of us. Just the same, I was up
and working by five o'clock this morning.

REGINE

All right, so now clear off. (*Pushes him.*) I'm not
having you in here. Out.

ENGSTRAND

Don't you worry, I'll be gone soon enough. We'll be
finished down the orphanage mid-day, then it's on the
boat and back to town for me …

REGINE

(*Mutters*) Good riddance.

ENGSTRAND

What with all the drinking for the opening, I'm better
off out of it. They're not going to say Jakob Engstrand
can't say no.

REGINE

Hah!

ENGSTRAND

Damned if I need him after me, the Reverend. Not just
now.

REGINE

Why, what are you up to?

ENGSTRAND

Up to?

REGINE

With the Pastor.

ENGSTRAND

Me? With Pastor Manders? Nothing! He's been a very good friend to me. That's what I want to talk to you about. (*She shoves him.*) No, now. I shall be off today.

REGINE

The sooner the better.

ENGSTRAND

What's more, you'll be coming with me.

REGINE

(*Her mouth open*) What?!

ENGSTRAND

I need you back home.

REGINE

With you? Not likely.

ENGSTRAND

We'll see about that.

REGINE

Oh, we will. I live here, with Mrs Alving. I'm treated like one of the family! You want me back with you, to a place like that?

ENGSTRAND

Listen to me, I'm your father, you bitch.

REGINE

(*Mutters*) No you're not. You didn't want to know me.

ENGSTRAND

Never mind that.

REGINE

All I got from you was names … dirty names.

ENGSTRAND

I've never used bad language to you.

REGINE

I haven't forgotten what you called me.

ENGSTRAND

Only when I was drunk …

REGINE

Ugh.

ENGSTRAND

… and when your mother got nasty. (*Mimics, in mock refinement*) 'Don't touch me, Engstrand. I'm in service to Chamberlain Alving at Rosenvold!' The Captain made a Chamberlain … oh, oh! (*Laughs*) If they only knew.

REGINE

You bullied the life out of her.

ENGSTRAND

Oh yes. All my fault.

REGINE

(*Mutters, turning away*) And that foot!

ENGSTRAND

What?

REGINE

Pied de mouton. *(Badly pronounced.)*

ENGSTRAND

What was that ... French?

REGINE

*(Sarcastic)* Hungarian.

ENGSTRAND

Good. It'll come in handy.

REGINE

*(Slight pause)* So, what do you want me for?

ENGSTRAND

You don't need to ask, do you? I'm a poor old widower, I'm lonely.

REGINE

Rubbish. What do you want?

ENGSTRAND

All right. I'll tell you. I've had an idea.

REGINE

Not another one?

ENGSTRAND

Ah, but this time. You wait. Regine, it's a damned good ...

REGINE

*(Stamps)* Stop it. I won't have swearing under this roof.

ENGSTRAND

Sssh! No, you're right, you're right. I just wanted to say, I've done well out of this orphanage work.

REGINE

Have you!

ENGSTRAND

Well, there's nothing to spend it on out here, is there?

REGINE

So?

ENGSTRAND

A hotel for seamen! (*REGINE snorts*) A proper, well-run place. Not just a pig-hole for sailors. For mates, ships' captains. First-class people.

REGINE

What do you want me for?

ENGSTRAND

To help. Be there. You wouldn't have to work hard. It could be as you want.

REGINE

(*Sarcastic*) Oh yes, I daresay.

ENGSTRAND

You must have women. A bit of life in the evenings. Singing, dancing – that sort of thing. These are seamen. They've been out there. (*Comes closer*) Now don't be silly, Regine. What's the point of hanging on here? All these books – what good's that going to do you? You don't want to run an orphanage. Surround yourself with snivelling brats?

REGINE

There are other things.

ENGSTRAND

What?

REGINE

Never mind. None of your business. How much have
you made on this job?

ENGSTRAND

Eight hundred kroner.

REGINE

Not bad.

ENGSTRAND

Enough to get me going, girl.

REGINE

What about some for me?

ENGSTRAND

Ho no!

REGINE

At least send me a length of cloth for a new dress.

ENGSTRAND

Come back to town with me, you can have as many
dresses as you want.

REGINE

I can manage that on my own.

ENGSTRAND

You'd do better with me behind you. I've seen a
nice house. Little Harbour Street – just right for a
seamen's hotel.

REGINE

I've told you – no! I'm not coming with you. I don't
want to stay with you, ever. So you can clear off.

ENGSTRAND

It would only be for a while. You've turned out a good-
looking girl. In no time at all, you'll meet some ship's
officer. A captain even.

REGINE

I'm not marrying a sailor.

ENGSTRAND

Why not?

REGINE

They ain't got no savoir-faire.

ENGSTRAND

What?

REGINE

Anyway, I know all about sailors. They're not the
marrying kind.

ENGSTRAND

All right, forget about being married. The other
way can work even better. (*Confidentially*) That
Englishman, remember? The one with the yacht? He
paid three hundred kroner. Three hundred! And she
was no better looking than you or your mother.

REGINE

(*Advances*) Get out of here ... get out!

ENGSTRAND

(*Steps back*) Don't you hit me.

REGINE

Mention my mother again, I will! Go on. Out of it! (*She
pushes him to the door*) And don't slam the door. Mr
Alving's ...

ENGSTRAND

I know, he's asleep. You worry about him all right.
(*Softer*) ... eh, it's not him you're ...?

REGINE

Out! No, not that way! (*She gives him a push.*) Down
the kitchen stairs. I don't want the Pastor to see you.

ENGSTRAND

All right, I'm going. But you talk to him. Honour thy
father, he'll tell you. And that's me. You want proof,
it's in the parish register!

ENGSTRAND goes.

REGINE tidies herself quickly, then goes to a bowl of flowers and
arranges them.

PASTOR MANDERS, in an overcoat, with an umbrella and a bag on
his shoulder, comes through garden door.

MANDERS

Miss Engstrand? Good morning.

REGINE

Ohh! It's the Pastor! Is the boat in already?

MANDERS

(*Comes into the room.*) Good morning, Regine.
Dreadful weather.

REGINE

But a blessing for the farmers, Pastor.

MANDERS

Yes, of course. We townsfolk forget that.

He starts to take off his coat.

REGINE

Can I help?

She helps him off with his coat.

REGINE

Oh Pastor! Your coat – all wet. Let me hang it in the hall. Shall I take your umbrella? I'll leave it open to dry.

She goes off with the things. MANDERS sets his bag and hat down as REGINE returns.

MANDERS

It's very good to be indoors. So, is everything going well out here?

REGINE

Yes, thank you.

MANDERS

And you're all run off your feet getting ready for tomorrow, eh?

REGINE

Oh, we are, sir.

MANDERS

Is Mrs Alving at home?

REGINE

Oh yes. She went upstairs with a hot drink for the young master.

MANDERS

I heard, down at the pier, that Osvald had arrived.

ACT ONE

REGINE

The day before yesterday. We didn't expect him till today!

MANDERS

All well, I trust?

REGINE

Yes, he's fine, thank you. Just ever so tired after the journey. He came all the way from Paris without a break! He's having a little sleep, I think, so we'll keep our voices down.

MANDERS

(*Dropped voice*) Yes, of course.

REGINE

(*Turns an armchair for the PASTOR*) Sit down, Pastor. Let me make you comfortable. (*She puts a stool under his feet.*) There, is that better?

MANDERS

Thank you. You know, Miss Engstrand, you've grown since I last saw you.

REGINE

I have. Mrs Alving says I'm filling out.

MANDERS

Perhaps a little. It becomes you.

A short pause.

REGINE

Shall I tell Mrs Alving you're here?

MANDERS

No hurry, dear child. Now, Regine, what news of your father? All in order there?

REGINE

Pretty much.

MANDERS

He came to see me when he was last in town.

REGINE

Oh, he's always pleased when he can talk to you,
Pastor.

MANDERS

You've been keeping an eye on him, I daresay, while
he's been out here. Have you managed to see him
every day?

REGINE

Every day?

MANDERS

Your father is not a strong character, Miss
Engstrand. He requires constant guidance.

REGINE

I know.

MANDERS

He needs someone by him, under his roof. Someone
whose judgement he respects. That man had the
honesty to admit as much, the last time he was in my
house.

REGINE

I know. He said so. But I can hardly leave Mrs Alving,
with the new orphanage to see to. She's been ever so
kind to me. I should hate to leave her.

MANDERS

Nonetheless, my dear girl, a daughter's duty, eh? We'd
need Mrs Alving's consent, of course.

REGINE

I don't think it would be right for me to keep house for
a single man – not at my age.

MANDERS

We're talking about your father, Miss Engstrand.

REGINE

That's as may be. It would be different if . . . if it were a
different sort of house . . . a gentleman's house.

MANDERS

Regine . . .

REGINE

Someone I could look up to, as a daughter.

MANDERS

My dear child . . .

REGINE

Of course, I'd like to live in town. It's lonely here. You
know what it's like to be alone in the world, Pastor.
I'm capable, and very willing. Do you know of such a
place for me?

MANDERS

I?

REGINE

In town . . . with a gentleman.

MANDERS

I'm afraid I don't.

REGINE

You will think of me, dear Mr Manders, if ever …

MANDERS

(*Rising*) Yes, yes.

REGINE

Because I do need …

MANDERS

Tell Mrs Alving I'm here if you will.

REGINE

Of course.

REGINE goes.

MANDERS paces, looks outside, then lifts a book from the table. He is surprised by it, and picks up others.

MANDERS

(*Murmurs*) We-ell …

MRS ALVING enters, followed by REGINE, who crosses and exits.

MRS ALVING

(*Extending her hand*) Pastor. So good to see you.

MANDERS

Mrs Alving. Here I am, as promised.

MRS ALVING

Punctual as ever.

MANDERS

Never easy, getting away, as you can imagine. So many boards and committees …

MRS ALVING

Then I'm all the more obliged to you. Where are your things?

MANDERS

(*Quickly*) I left them down at the harbour. I'm staying there for the night.

MRS ALVING

(*Smiling*) I can't persuade you to spend even one night here?

MANDERS

It's convenient to be near the boat.

MRS ALVING

Well, do as you wish. But, really, two old people like us ...

MANDERS

Oh, you will have your little joke, Mrs Alving. You're in fine spirits today. Well, the celebration tomorrow. Your son home.

MRS ALVING

After two years ... yes, I'm very happy. He's promised to stay for the winter!

MANDERS

Very good of him. Especially with all those attractions in Paris.

MRS ALVING

But he has his mother here. The dear boy still has room for me.

MANDERS

I'm happy to hear that devotion to art, and the like, hasn't blunted his natural feelings.

MRS ALVING

Oh, there's no chance of that. I wonder, will you still
recognize him? He'll be down in a minute. He's just
having a rest. But now … dear Pastor … do sit down.

MANDERS

Is this a convenient time to discuss business?

MRS ALVING

Of course. *(She sits at the table.)*

MANDERS

*(Gets papers, and sits across from her.)* Let's have a
look, shall we? *(Breaks off)* Oh, by the way, where did
these come from?

MRS ALVING

The books? I'm reading them.

MANDERS

You read this sort of thing?

MRS ALVING

Why yes.

MANDERS

I see. Do you feel the better for it?

MRS ALVING

I feel more secure, yes.

MANDERS

How surprising. In what way?

MRS ALVING

They reinforce ideas, thoughts of my own. Things
that I'm sure we all think, but don't talk about.
Perhaps because we prefer not to face them.

MANDERS

You can't seriously believe that most people are like
that.

MRS ALVING

I do, yes.

MANDERS

Our sort of people?

MRS ALVING

Oh yes. *(Touches the books)* Show me what you object
to.

MANDERS

I'm afraid I don't waste my time on that kind of
publication.

MRS ALVING

So, you don't know what you're condemning?

MANDERS

I've read enough about this sort of thing to
disapprove thoroughly of . . .

MRS ALVING

But your opinions are not first hand?

MANDERS

My dear Mrs Alving, there are many occasions in life
where one has to rely on the opinions of others. That
is how society functions.

MRS ALVING

You're probably right.

MANDERS

I don't deny a certain fascination. And I don't blame
you for being interested in current intellectual ideas

in the world out there. Where your son ... where
you've allowed your son to ... However, perhaps the
less said the better. All the same, reading within
one's four walls is one thing, but you have special
obligations.

MRS ALVING

Obligations?

MANDERS

To the orphanage. Which you decided to found at
a time when your spiritual values perhaps were
somewhat different from those you now seem to ...
However, that's just the way I see it.

MRS ALVING

Exactly. But it was about the Refuge, the
Orphanage ...

MANDERS

... that we wanted to talk, yes. Just the same –
discretion, my dear Mrs Alving, I beg of you. Now, to
business. *(Opens folder.)*

MRS ALVING

Ah, the deeds!

MANDERS

Everything is in order. It hasn't been easy. The
authorities are almost painfully conscientious
when it comes to making decisions. However, I
have managed to push things through. Here is the
conveyance of the plot and the new buildings, which
comprise the school, staff quarters and chapel. And
this is the official charter, together with the bye-
laws that will govern the running of the orphanage.

ACT ONE

(*Reads*) 'Bye-laws governing the Captain Alving
Memorial Orphanage and Refuge.'

MRS ALVING takes the papers and looks at them for a long
moment.

MRS ALVING

So, here it is.

MANDERS

I put Captain rather than Court Chamberlain, it
seemed less ostentatious.

MRS ALVING

Whatever you think best.

MANDERS

The bankbook, showing interest on capital set aside
for running expenses ...

MRS ALVING

Oh please, won't you take care of that?

MANDERS

As you wish. We may as well leave the money on
deposit for the time being. I know the interest's very
low – four per cent – and you have to wait six months
to make a withdrawal. Perhaps later on, if we could
lend it out as a mortgage ... a first mortgage, of
course, and absolutely secure – we might reconsider.

MRS ALVING

You know best.

MANDERS

I'll keep my eyes open. Now, one more matter.
Insurance.

MRS ALVING

Insurance?

MANDERS

Do you feel that we should insure the Orphanage?

MRS ALVING

Of course. Everything I own is insured. House,
furniture, crops, livestock ...

MANDERS

Naturally. With your own property. I do the same. But
this, d'you see, is a different matter. The Orphanage,
if I may remind you, is to be consecrated to a higher
purpose.

MRS ALVING

Well, yes, but all the same ...

MANDERS

From a personal point of view, I'd have not the least
objection to insuring against all risk. But we could be
accused of a lack of faith in Divine Providence, could
we not?

MRS ALVING

Is that likely? Surely, if we are satisfied in our own
minds ...

MANDERS

But what would be the general feeling? I mean
locally? Are there people, whose opinions matter, who
might take offence?

MRS ALVING

Well, perhaps, though hardly likely.

ACT ONE

MANDERS

(*Carrying on*) Other denominations and their
congregations for a start. I've seen it all before.

MRS ALVING

My dear Pastor ...

MANDERS

We must think beyond ourselves in this situation,
must we not? If we allow a false impression of our
motives to become public ... Should we convey an
interest in the mundane, might not that hamper the
good works that we seek to achieve?

MRS ALVING

You feel that insuring everything is likely to do that?

MANDERS

There is also my own situation. One can hardly shut
one's eyes to the difficult, one might almost say
painful, position in which I might find myself. People
of influence in the town are extremely interested
in the orphanage. It is, after all, designed for civic
benefit. The burden of caring for the poor will most
certainly be lightened. As your adviser, I shall
undoubtedly be first in the line of fire from the more
bigoted elements, so to speak.

MRS ALVING

Surely not.

MANDERS

My name defiled in certain papers and journals, if
we are seen to be dispensing sums that might be
considered more properly used for succouring those
in need. I could even be accused of malpractice.

MRS ALVING

No, Mr Manders. I won't have that. No, no, no!

MANDERS

Then, shall we say ... ?

MRS ALVING

Let us forget the insurance.

MANDERS

Ah, but you see, if there should be an untoward occurrence ... after all, one can never be sure ... are you, Mrs Alving, that is to say, could you, would you be in a position to make up the loss?

MRS ALVING

I am afraid not.

MANDERS

Then we assume between us a grave responsibility.

MRS ALVING

What else can we do?

MANDERS

What indeed?

MRS ALVING

Especially you, given your calling.

MANDERS

Then we agree to rely on the benevolence of divine providence.

MRS ALVING

Yes indeed.

MANDERS

And leave things as they are?

She nods.

                    MANDERS

As you wish. (*Makes a note.*) No insurance.

                    MRS ALVING

Odd that you should mention it – insurance, I mean.

MANDERS looks up.

                    MRS ALVING

There was a fire yesterday.

                    MANDERS

What?

                    MRS ALVING

Oh, nothing to speak of. Just some shavings in the
carpenter's shop.

                    MANDERS

Engstrand, you mean?

                    MRS ALVING

Throwing down matches. I'm afraid he's very
careless.

                    MANDERS

A man of tribulations, Mrs Alving. But, I am happy to
report, on the way to a better and purer life.

                    MRS ALVING

Who says so?

                    MANDERS

He told me so himself. He's a good workman.

                    MRS ALVING

Oh indeed. When he's sober.

MANDERS

It's the leg, do you see? But he came to visit me when
he was in town. Just to thank me for getting him the
work here, so he could be with his daughter.

MRS ALVING

Regine? He never sees her!

MANDERS

Oh no, he talks to her every single day. He told me.

MRS ALVING

Really?

MANDERS

He feels he needs a restraining hand to keep him
from temptation. That is what is so very touching
about the man. His nakedness. Now, if it truly became
vital for him to have Regine home again . . .

MRS ALVING

(*Rises*) What?

MANDERS

You wouldn't set yourself against that?

MRS ALVING

I most certainly would.

MANDERS

He is her father, remember.

MRS ALVING

And what sort of a father? No, that would not have my
blessing.

MANDERS

(*Rising*) My dear Mrs Alving. Please don't upset
yourself. I can't think why the man alarms you.
Believe me, you misjudge him.

MRS ALVING

(*More calmly*) Be that as it may. What matters is that
I've taken Regine into my home. And here she stays.
(*Listens*) Sssh! We'll say no more. (*Smiles, happy*)
Osvald's coming down … There's Osvald to talk
about!

OSVALD ALVING, wearing a light overcoat, hat in hand, and
smoking a large meerschaum pipe, enters.

OSVALD

(*In the doorway*) I'm sorry, I thought you were in the
study. Good morning, Pastor Manders.

MANDERS

(*Stares at him*) Ah! Astonishing! …

MRS ALVING

Well! What do you think of him. Pastor?

MANDERS

I … no … Can it really be … ?

OSVALD

Yes. The Prodigal Son.

MANDERS

My dear boy …

OSVALD

Well, the son anyway.

**MRS ALVING**

I daresay Osvald's thinking of the way you so strongly objected to his becoming a painter, do you remember?

**MANDERS**

Many a step that looks doubtful at the time ... At all events, welcome home, Osvald. You'll allow me to call you by that name?

**OSVALD**

What else?

**MANDERS**

What I meant to say, my dear Osvald ... what I mean to convey ... I don't condemn the life of the artist out of hand. Not in the least. I daresay there are more than a few who manage to keep themselves free from corruption and temptation.

**OSVALD**

No doubt.

**MRS ALVING**

(*Smiling*) One for sure. You've only to look at him, Pastor!

**OSVALD**

Yes, all right, Mother, that's enough.

**MRS ALVING**

And he's making a name for himself. The name Osvald Alving is often in the Paris papers.

**OSVALD**

Not so much recently. I haven't been painting.

MRS ALVING

Even artists need to stop now and then.

MANDERS

A pause ... for contemplation, and to prepare for the
great works to come.

OSVALD

When is lunch?

MRS ALVING

In half an hour. He has a wonderful appetite, thank
the Lord.

MANDERS

And likes his tobacco too, I see.

OSVALD

I found this *(waves the pipe)* upstairs, in the bedroom.

MANDERS

Ah, then that explains it!

MRS ALVING

I'm sorry?

MANDERS

When you came down those stairs I saw your father.

OSVALD

Oh?

MRS ALVING

I don't know how you can say that. Osvald takes after
me.

MANDERS

But there's a look, d'you see? Around the corners of
the mouth. Something about the lips. Now, with the

pipe in his mouth, he's the very image of Captain Alving.

MRS ALVING

Not at all. Nothing like him. Osvald has more the look of a minister of the church.

MANDERS

Perhaps that's what I was seeing.

MRS ALVING

Dearest, I'd rather you didn't smoke in here.

OSVALD

(Puts the pipe down) I just wanted to try it. I did once before, when I was a child.

MRS ALVING

Did you?

OSVALD

When I was little, I went into Father's room. I remember it very well. He was in a marvellous mood.

MRS ALVING

You can't possibly remember.

OSVALD

I do. He took me on his knee and let me smoke his pipe. 'Smoke, my boy!' he said. 'Smoke it for real!' I sucked right in as far as I could, till the sweat fell off my forehead. He laughed so much.

MANDERS

Laughed?

MRS ALVING

You just dreamed it.

OSVALD

No, Mother, don't you remember? You came in and carried me off to the nursery to be sick. I remember you were crying. Did he often play tricks like that?

MANDERS

A man full of life, your father.

OSVALD

And did so much in spite of dying young.

MANDERS

You've inherited a worthy name, Osvald. Pray God it will be an inspiration to you.

OSVALD

Yes.

MANDERS

We're so grateful to have you here to honour your father's memory.

OSVALD

The least I could do.

MRS ALVING

And he's staying!

MANDERS

I hear you're at home for the winter.

OSVALD

Yes, indefinitely. Oh, it's good to be home!

MRS ALVING

Yes!

MANDERS

After being out in the world so early.

MRS ALVING

Nonsense! There's nothing better for a healthy young man, especially when he's an only child. No use staying at home to be coddled.

MANDERS

A debatable proposition, if I may say so, Mrs Alving. A child's proper place must always be his father's house.

OSVALD

I agree.

MANDERS

Look at Osvald. I think we can say this in front of him. Here we have a young man of twenty-six who's never yet had the chance of a real home of his own.

OSVALD

No, that's not true.

MANDERS

Oh? I thought you moved entirely in artistic circles?

OSVALD

Yes, that's so.

MANDERS

Among younger artists?

OSVALD inclines his head.

OSVALD

Yes.

MANDERS

Who don't, I assume, have the means to build a home, start a family . . . ?

OSVALD

They can't afford to marry. But they still have a home life, some of them.

MRS ALVING following attentively, nods.

MANDERS

No, no, I wasn't talking of a bachelor establishment. I mean a family home, where a man lives with his wife, his children.

OSVALD

That's what I meant. A man with his children and their mother.

MANDERS

In the name of our merciful father!

OSVALD

I'm sorry?

MANDERS

Lives? With the mother of his children? You mean without the sanction of marriage?

OSVALD

What do you want him to do? Abandon them?

MANDERS

But you're talking of illicit relations! What you describe is nothing more nor less than wicked and irresponsible Free Love!

OSVALD

I can't say I've noticed any particular irresponsibility.

MANDERS

But how could any decently brought up young man or
woman accept such a way of life?

OSVALD

What else can they do? They've no money, no means.
What can they do?

MANDERS

What can they do? I'll tell you what they can do, Mr
Alving. They can keep one another at a distance.
That's what they can do!

OSVALD

When they're in love?

MRS ALVING

Yes, what then?

MANDERS

I am shocked. To think that the authorities allow such
wantonness to go on openly. *(To MRS ALVING)* Now
you see how right I was to be concerned about Osvald.
To be exposed to circles where immorality is not only
permitted but accepted -

OSVALD

Pastor, please. I've been a frequent Sunday visitor to
more than one of these ... unconventional ...

MANDERS

On a Sunday?!

OSVALD

Yes, a day to enjoy. And never once have I heard
anything untoward. Shall I tell you where I <u>have</u> met
immorality? From husbands and fathers away from

home, out to see life in the artists' cafes. If you want
to know about sin, ask them.

MANDERS

Are you suggesting that respectable men from
here ... ?

OSVALD

You'll have heard them talking about the loose morals
of foreigners. These respectable travelled citizens
when they come home. How do they know, eh? Believe
me, they know because they have had first-hand
experience. Who is it who fouls the life of the artist?
The genuine free life. I'll tell you ...

MRS ALVING

Osvald, don't. Please don't upset yourself. It's bad for
you.

OSVALD

Yes, you're right. It's this damned fatigue. I'll go for a
walk before lunch. Forgive me, Pastor, I don't expect
you share my feelings, but I know what I'm talking
about. For vice, there must be patrons of vice.

OSVALD goes out.

MRS ALVING

My poor, dear boy ...

MANDERS

Well said. Well said indeed. Now we see how far he's
strayed!

He paces.

MRS ALVING says nothing.

MANDERS

You notice that he calls himself the prodigal son?
Very sad. Very sad.

MRS ALVING does not answer.

MANDERS

What have you to say now, Mrs Alving?

MRS ALVING

(*Pause*) He›s right. I agree with what he says.

MANDERS

You agree? With slanderous nonsense? With loose
and immoral principles?

MRS ALVING

Not with immorality, no. My quarrel is with the so-
called morality that is merely a cloak for darkness.
And for the so-called morality that denies the young
expression. Of course, I've never dared open my
mouth. Not until now. Now Osvald is here he can
speak for me.

MANDERS

If these are indeed your thoughts, then you are
to be pitied. We need to talk seriously. (*He paces.*)
Mrs Alving, I speak to you now not as you and your
husband's childhood friend but as your priest.

MRS ALVING

Priest?

MANDERS

As I did once before at a particular moment in your
life.

MRS ALVING

(*Quietly*) And what does my priest have to say?

MANDERS

Let me take you back. Tomorrow is the tenth
anniversary of your husband's death. The day that
a memorial will be unveiled in his honour. A day
when I shall be speaking from the platform to a large
company of people. Today I speak to you alone.

MRS ALVING

Pray do.

MANDERS

(*Pause*) Do you remember how, after one year of
marriage, you stood on the edge of a chasm? How
you left your home. Deserted your husband? Yes,
Mrs Alving, deserted him! You refused, you utterly
refused to go back, despite his pleadings and sorrow.

MRS ALVING

I was in despair. Have you forgotten that? How
unhappy I was?

MANDERS

But can't you see? Out of your own mouth! This is
the very heart of the rebellious spirit. Who are we
to crave happiness in this life? Do we have a right to
joy? What right? No Mrs Alving. We are here to obey,
to submit, and to do our duty. Your duty was to stand
by the man of your choice. The man to whom you were
bound by sacred vows. Your husband.

MRS ALVING

But you knew the life he was leading – where his
desires were taking him.

MANDERS

There were rumours, yes. If they were true, such
conduct was unacceptable. But was it your role to
be your husband's judge? Was not your duty as his
wife to bear the cross that providence saw fit to lay
on your shoulders? Instead, you chose to cast off the
burdens of a Higher Will. You reneged on your sacred
task. You saw fit to abandon the soul most close to
you, most in need of succour. You left, risking your
name. The good name of your family. Not to mention
the good name of others.

MRS ALVING

One other, I believe you mean.

MANDERS

And did you not think, when you came to me? Did you
not consider?

MRS ALVING

I came to an old family friend. To my Pastor.

MANDERS

And thank the Almighty that I had the strength,
that it was given to me to make you see the light and
to lead you back to your duty and the hearth of your
lawful spouse.

MRS ALVING

Yes. That was certainly your doing.

MANDERS

As the humble instrument of a Higher Power. With
God's help, I bent your will to obedience and all the
blessings that followed. It went as I foretold. Did not
your husband, as I promised, give up the life he was

leading? Was there ever a more decent and upright man, right until the end? A man created Court Chamberlain A benefactor to the whole community, with you at his side, supporting him – sharing! I witnessed that sharing, Mrs Alving, and your tireless contribution. It is to your credit, and I am the first – the very first to attest to that. But then there was your second mistake.

MRS ALVING

Mistake? What do you mean?

MANDERS

Just as you had sought to evade your duties as a wife you then – it grieves me to say this – chose to evade your central and most sacred duty as a mother.

MRS ALVING

Ahh!

MANDERS

Again, the sin of disobedience. Willfulness! You have a spirit in you that draws you to that which is unrestrained, undisciplined. You hate to be confined. Carelessly and irresponsibly, you cast aside that which impedes or inconveniences you. It didn't suit you to be a wife, so you left. You deserted your husband. You found it tiresome, restricting, to be a mother, and so you abandoned your child and left him to strangers.

MRS ALVING

Yes, I did that.

MANDERS

So that now he is a stranger to you.

MRS ALVING

No.

MANDERS

How can it not be so? And what sort of son is he,
now that we see him? You failed your husband, the
very raising of this monument to him betrays your
feelings of guilt. Admit it. Find the strength to face
the truth that you have failed, too, your son. There
may still be time. It may be possible to claw him back
from the paths of error into righteousness, if you are
prepared to change yourself, become fit and able to
save what is left of that boy. You, and you alone, are to
blame. As a wife – and as a mother. It is the duty of my
calling to tell you this.

Silence.

MRS ALVING

(Calmly, controlling herself) You have had your
say, Pastor Manders. Tomorrow you will be on the
platform, speaking in public of my husband's memory.
Tomorrow I shall be silent. I shall make no speeches. I
shall speak now. As you have chosen to speak to me.

MANDERS

No doubt to seek to make excuses for your conduct. I
am prepared to . . .

MRS ALVING

No. I wish merely to state some facts.

MANDERS

Very well. I am listening.

MRS ALVING

Everything that you've said about my husband and
me. About our ... our life together. After you sent
me ... led me back to, as you call it, the path of duty ...
You know nothing of that life – our life. From the
moment I returned, you, who used to visit us every
day, never set foot in our house.

MANDERS

I moved away, almost at once.

MRS ALVING

That's true. And not once, while my husband was
alive, at any time did you take the trouble to come
and see us. The only reason that you have visited
recently is because of the orphanage – a business
matter.

MANDERS

(Low) Hélène. If that is meant as a reproach to me
then I must ask you to consider ...

MRS ALVING

... the respect you owed to your calling, yes. I was
a woman who had run away from her husband. You
can't be too careful with women like that.

MANDERS

Please ... you exaggerate. My dear Mrs Alving ...

MRS ALVING

We'll forget I said that. I simply want you to know
that, when you judge my married life, you can only be
making a judgement on hearsay.

MANDERS

That may be so.

MRS ALVING

And now I shall tell you the truth. I promised myself
that one day – one day you at least should be told.

MANDERS

And pray what is it that you have to tell me.

MRS ALVING

The truth is that my husband did not change his way
of life. He lived as … as he had always done … until
the day he died.

MANDERS

What?

MRS ALVING

For nineteen years, during all the years of our
marriage, my husband lived what you would call a
dissolute life. The life he had lived before you married
us.

MANDERS

But these early indiscretions – the follies of youth –
you call these dissolute?

MRS ALVING

It is the word used by my doctor.

MANDERS

I'm sorry, I don't understand.

MRS ALVING

You don't need to.

MANDERS

Are you saying that your marriage was a mockery all
those years?

MRS ALVING

Yes.

MANDERS

I ... I find that very hard to believe. No, it doesn't
make sense. It would all come out! A secret life here?
No, no, no ...

MRS ALVING

Oh, it's perfectly possible. A man of such charm – so
likeable, everyone said. I thought, after Osvald was
born ... but no. I had to fight even harder to keep his
reputation intact. I was his willing accomplice. That
is, until he brought his way of life into this house.

MANDERS

What? Brought what?

MRS ALVING

There was a relationship with one of the maids.
"Please, Captain, please!" Night after night.
Ludicrous.

MANDERS

Totally unacceptable. But, with young girls about the
house, no more than high spirits, surely?

MRS ALVING

The affair had consequences, Pastor Manders.

MANDERS

Consequences? You mean she ... ?

MRS ALVING

Yes. She gave birth. Here. Upstairs. In this house.

MANDERS

And you are saying that you permitted this
wickedness? Under your own roof?

MRS ALVING

At that time, I was prepared to endure anything. His
fists, violence – anything – just to keep him at home,
where I thought I could restrain him. He took his
amusements anyway. At least it gave me a weapon –
something to blackmail him with. I provided for the
woman, cared for the child – she was my son's half-
sister! And took control of the house and our affairs.
But I had to send Osvald away. (Her voice breaks.)
How could I keep him here? He was beginning to see
things. He even tried to protect me. Oh, you can't
know what it cost me to let him go!

MANDERS

Dreadful.

MRS ALVING

I survived by working. All the improvements to the
farm and properties – everything that Alving was
praised for. Did you honestly believe they were his
doing? He lay on a sofa, day and night. There were
moments of lucidity, but always the relapse into
delirium. Days of coma … rage … weeping …

MANDERS

And this is the man to whom you are raising a
monument?

MRS ALVING

What better way to hide the truth?

MANDERS

You have certainly succeeded in that.

MRS ALVING

I had another reason. I want Osvald to inherit
nothing from his father.

MANDERS

So, the money ...

MRS ALVING

The exact amount that made Lieutenant Alving such
a good match has been spent on the orphanage. Every
last kroner. When Osvald inherits, it will be from me.
My money.

OSVALD comes in.

MRS ALVING

Ah, you're back, my dear.

OSVALD

What can one do? This endless rain! But I hear lunch
is ready. That's good.

REGINE enters with a package.

REGINE

A parcel for you, ma'am.

MRS ALVING

The choir music for tomorrow I daresay.

MANDERS

Mmm.

REGINE

Dinner's ready ... I mean, lunch is served.

MRS ALVING

(*Opening the package.*) We'll be along in a moment.

REGINE

Will Mr Alving have red or white, ma'am?

OSVALD

Both, Regine!

REGINE

Bien. Very good, Mr Alving.

OSVALD

I'll come and help you uncork.

They go into the dining room.

MRS ALVING

Yes, it's the sheet music for the choir.

MANDERS

How shall I ever be able to give my speech tomorrow?
What am I going to say?

MRS ALVING

Oh, you'll manage.

MANDERS

(*Low*) No scandal, please, I beg of you.

MRS ALVING

(*Firm*) After tomorrow the farce will be over. It will
be just my son and me. Just the two of us.

The sound of a chair knocked over.

REGINE's voice, in a sharp whisper.

REGINE

Osvald, are you mad? Stop it!

MRS ALVING is rigid, her face white.

MRS ALVING

Ah!

She stares at the door, as if mesmerised.

OSVALD coughs, and starts humming. The sound of a bottle being uncorked.

MANDERS

What's the matter, Mrs Alving? What is it?

MRS ALVING

(*Hoarse*) Ghosts. Don't you understand? Regine! She's the ... the ...

MANDERS

Regine? You meant that Regine ... she's the ...?

MRS ALVING

Not a word, do you understand? Not a word!

She grips his arm fiercely for support, and moves shakily towards the dining room.

*Fade to black.*

ACT TWO

The room as before. A mist over the landscape beyond.

MRS ALVING and PASTOR MANDERS enter from the dining room.

MRS ALVING

(*Towards the dining room*) Osvald, are you joining
us?

OSVALD

(*Off*) No, thanks. I'm going out for a while.

MRS ALVING

Why not? I think it's clearing up a little.

MRS ALVING closes the door to the dining room, and crosses to
the hall.

MRS ALVING

(*Calls*) Regine!

REGINE

(*Off*) Yes, ma'am?

MRS ALVING

Would you go down to the wash-house and give them a
hand with the decorations?

REGINE

I will, ma'am.

MRS ALVING pauses, to make sure REGINE is out of earshot, and
shuts the door.

MANDERS

Your son can't hear us?

MRS ALVING

No – he's gone out.

MANDERS

How I managed to sit through lunch I'll never know!

She paces. And stops before him.

MRS ALVING

So. What is to be done?

MANDERS

What indeed? I've no experience in these matters.

MRS ALVING

Have you not? I thought they were your forte. Surely the preservation of virtue comes within your sphere? However, as to that, nothing serious has happened. Osvald has just taken a passing fancy to her.

MANDERS

It must be stopped. She must be removed at once.

MRS ALVING

I can't simply turn her out of the house. This is her home. Where would she go?

MANDERS

Back to her father, of course.

MRS ALVING

Her father?

MANDERS

Yes! Oh, but of course he isn't her father. Mrs Alving, how can this be? You can't be right! Are you sure?

MRS ALVING

That Regine is? Oh yes. Johanna, my maid, came to me for help. And Alving didn't deny the relationship. There was nothing to be done but have the whole thing hushed up.

MANDERS

I see.

MRS ALVING

Johanna was sent off with enough money to hold her tongue – and managed very well for herself. She took up with Engstrand, told him some story about a foreigner on a yacht. Anyway, they were married – well, you married them yourself.

MANDERS

I remember, quite distinctly, the day Engstrand came to see me. He was full of remorse. Accused himself bitterly for the way he and the young woman – his fiancée as he called her – had ... stepped ahead of themselves, so to speak.

MRS ALVING

So he took on the blame?

MANDERS

The hypocrisy of it! And to me! I would never have believed such a thing of Jakob Engstrand. The immorality of such a marriage! And for money! How much did she get?

MRS ALVING

Three hundred kroner.

MANDERS

Three hundred? Can you imagine it? Tying himself
to a degraded woman for a miserable three hundred
kroner!

MRS ALVING

Then your poor opinion must extend to me, Pastor.

MANDERS

What?

MRS ALVING

I also married into degradation. When I stood at the
altar with Alving, was he any worthier?

MANDERS

Nonsense. There's a world of difference.

MRS ALVING

A difference in price, yes. Between three hundred
kroner and a sizeable fortune.

MANDERS

There's no comparison.

MRS ALVING

Isn't there?

MANDERS

You listened to the loving advice of your family. And
to the dictates of your own heart.

MRS ALVING

(*Looks away from him*) Oh, I think you know where
my heart was at that time. And to whom I had lost it.

MANDERS

Had I known that, I would never have been a visitor
to your husband's house.

MRS ALVING

At all events, whoever I listened to, it was not myself.

MANDERS

You listened to those closest to you, as was proper.

MRS ALVING

Was it? They wrote up my bill of sale, that's for sure.
Interest on capital invested ... estimated gain ...
Madness to turn down such a profitable offer. Not to
mention disobedient. If my mother could see what all
the promise and splendour came to! Well, at least she
never knew.

MANDERS

No-one can foresee how a marriage will work out.
No-one should be blamed. Your marriage took place in
good faith, and with proper respect for the law.

MRS ALVING

(Sighs) Respect for the law? The cause of most of the
mischief in this world, I sometimes think.

MANDERS

Now that, if I may say so, Mrs Alving, is a very sinful
statement.

MRS ALVING

Possibly. All I know is that I am still chained
by obligation. Conventions that I perceive to be
unreasonable. I want to be free.

MANDERS

Free? From what?

MRS ALVING

(Drumming her fingers) I should never have covered
it up. Any of it. The drink, the violence, the cruelty. I

was a coward. Yes, I did it for Osvald – but it was also for my own benefit. Oh yes.

MANDERS

In what way? If you say your husband was a monster . . .

MRS ALVING

Should I have left him? If I had, who would have taken the blame? 'Poor man. Deserted by a faithless woman who abandons her vows.' Isn't that so?

MANDERS

I daresay. I daresay.

MRS ALVING

I should have told Osvald the truth. I should have looked him in the face and said: 'My son, your father is a degenerate, drunken, lying, lascivious . . .'

MANDERS

Stop it!

MRS ALVING

I should have told him everything. As I'm telling you now. What is it? What's the matter?

MANDERS

(Shakes his head.) Nothing. You scare me.

MRS ALVING

I scare myself sometimes. When I allow myself to think – which, fortunately, isn't often. You see, I'm a coward.

MANDERS

How can it be cowardice to do your duty? To protect a
child so that he may love and honour his father, and
his mother, as he is enjoined to do.

MRS ALVING

Oh, Pastor! These are abstractions! Is it right that
Osvald should be made to love and respect a man such
as Alving?

MANDERS

Is it right that a mother should seek to destroy the
innocence and happiness of her only child?

MRS ALVING

At the expense of truth?

MANDERS

In order to preserve his ideals.

MRS ALVING

Oh – ideals.

MANDERS

Don't destroy those, Mrs Alving. That is cruel. Very
cruel indeed. Osvald, it appears, does not have the
protection of inherited principles. He wavers. Leave
him, at least, with respect and love for his father.

MRS ALVING

Yes ...

MANDERS

You've created a beautiful and nourishing image. Do
not, I beg of you, destroy that.

Silence.

MRS ALVING

And Regine?

MANDERS

He mustn't go near her.

MRS ALVING

No. Mind you, if I thought it would make him happy,
I'd say 'Marry her!'

MANDERS

What? In the name of God!

MRS ALVING

Why not?

MANDERS

This is sheer barbarity!

MRS ALVING

Not at all. I'm serious. You know very well, Pastor,
how many families out here are more than closely
related.

MANDERS

I'm sorry. I don't know what you mean.

MRS ALVING

Yes, you do. You understand very well.

MANDERS

Some families aren't as ... as they should be. But it's
not usual. As far as we know. What you are saying,
Mrs Alving, is that you – an educated and responsible
woman, would be willing to allow your own son ...

MRS ALVING

Not willing. Unwilling. But only because I'm a coward.
Besides, aren't we all descended from the one original
union? And whose idea was that?

MANDERS

This is blasphemy. I will not discuss such questions
with you in your present state. To cite cowardice as
the only obstacle to abomination!

MRS ALVING

Please. You don't understand. When I say I'm a
coward, I mean I'm afraid.

MANDERS

Afraid of what?

MRS ALVING

Ghosts.

MANDERS

Ghosts? What ghosts?

MRS ALVING

When I heard them in there just now, *(She shudders)*
I almost believed that we're all ghosts. All of us. It's
not only what we inherit from our fathers, mothers,
grandparents ... It's every kind of dead belief inside
us. Pick up a newspaper, a journal. Every line – or,
in- between the lines – ghosts! Like grains of sand,
clogging the arteries. Or black forest canopies,
keeping the light from us. How <u>can</u> we be brave – see
things as they are – when our eyes are webbed with
weed ... misted over?

MANDERS

This is the result of your reading those insidious,
free-thinking books.

MRS ALVING

No. It was you who started me thinking. And for that I
shall always be grateful.

MANDERS

Me?

MRS ALVING

Yes. When you spent those hours and days
persuading me of my obligations. When you praised
to the skies what I felt, in my heart, to be loathsome
and untruthful. That's when I began to go over your
teachings, line by line, seam by seam, and pulled
at the threads. And the more I pulled, the more the
whole design fell apart.

MANDERS

Is that what I achieved, after the hardest fought
battle of my life?

MRS ALVING

Your most abject defeat, I think.

MANDERS

No. My greatest victory. Over myself.

MRS ALVING

On the contrary, it was a crime. Against both of us.

MANDERS

Because I said 'Woman, go home to your lawful
husband?' when you came to me, out of your mind,
saying: 'Here I am. Take me!' You call that a crime?

MRS ALVING

Yes, I think it was.

MANDERS

Then we don't understand each other.

MRS ALVING

Not now. Not anymore.

MANDERS

Never. Never in my most secret heart have I ever seen
you as anything other than another man's wife.

MRS ALVING

You expect me to believe that?

MANDERS

Hélène!

MRS ALVING

We forget so easily the people that we were.

MANDERS

Not I. I am the same. The same as I always was.

MRS ALVING

(Changes tone) I daresay. Well, that was then. This
is now. You are busy all the time with committees,
boards, speeches. And I sit here struggling with
ghosts.

MANDERS

I can help you. At least with some of them. For a start,
that young girl cannot remain in this house. If we
could find a husband for her ... Don't you think that
would be advisable?

MRS ALVING

Marry her off? (Ironic) Ah, yes.

MANDERS

Not without her full consent.

MRS ALVING

As you say.

MANDERS

She has reached the age when ...

MRS ALVING

She matured very early.

MANDERS

Yes, I noticed. Perhaps, for now, she should be sent
home to her father. To think how that man deceived
me! Claiming to be the girl's father. Nobly standing
at the side of the woman, after they had given way to
weakness together! Did he ...? Does he know her real
father?

A KNOCK at the hall door.

MRS ALVING

Now who is that?

ENGSTRAND appears in his Sunday clothes.

ENGSTRAND

I do beg your pardon, most humbly -

MANDERS

Oh, you is it?

MRS ALVING

Engstrand ...

ENGSTRAND

None of the maids was about, so I hope you don't
mind. I knocked on the door myself.

MRS ALVING

How can I help you?

ENGSTRAND

It was the Pastor, actually. I wanted a word.

MANDERS

(*Walking up and down*) Oh yes? Me, is it? It's me you
want, eh?

ENGSTRAND

I'd be ever so grateful.

MANDERS confronts him.

MANDERS

So, what is it?

ENGSTRAND

It's like this, you see, Pastor. We've all been paid
off. Thanks to you, ma'am. And everything being
all finished up. I thought how nice it would be if us
honest craftsmen ... If ... well, I was thinking if we
rounded it all off with a little prayer meeting tonight.

MANDERS

A prayer meeting?

ENGSTRAND

Down at the orphanage. Of course, if it's not
convenient ...

MANDERS

No, no. It's a fine idea.

ENGSTRAND

I've been holding a few evening prayers down there
myself ... just, you know ...

MRS ALVING

You?

ENGSTRAND

Now and then. A few quiet words together. I'm only
an ordinary bloke. Lord knows I'm nothing special . . .
but, anyway, I was thinking . . . with you being out
here with us . . .

MANDERS

Yes, yes, yes. Well, that's as may be. But there's
something I need to know, Engstrand. Tell me this. On
the matter of conscience, how is yours? Can you tell
me, in all honesty, that your conscience is clear?

ENGSTRAND

Oh now, Pastor, God help me. I mean, if we're talking
about conscience . . .

MANDERS

That is exactly what we're talking about. And I would
appreciate an answer.

ENGSTRAND

Conscience? Well, sir, as to that, I couldn't say. I
couldn't claim to be clear in my mind about that.

MANDERS

At least you've the grace not to lie to me. I am going to
ask you a question, and I want an honest answer. It is
about Regine.

ENGSTRAND

Regine? What's up with her?

MANDERS

Whose daughter is she?

MRS ALVING

Pastor Manders!

MANDERS

Leave it to me, Mrs Alving.

ENGSTRAND

My word, you gave me a turn! I thought you meant something had happened to her.

MANDERS

Would you be good enough to answer my question? Are you Regine's natural father? Or are you not?

ENGSTRAND

Well, as to that … you remember the business with me and my dear lost Johanna?

MANDERS

Don't prevaricate, man. Before your late wife left the service of this lady, she told Mrs Alving the truth … the truth, Engstrand.

ENGSTRAND

But it was supposed to be a secret. You mean she let on?

MANDERS

So, your secret is out, Engstrand.

ENGSTRAND

But she swore me to secrecy, didn't she? She made me promise.

MANDERS

And all these years you kept the truth from me? From me, your Pastor! I trusted you, and you lied to me!

ENGSTRAND

I'm sorry.

MANDERS

Did I deserve this? Haven't I always held out my hand
to you? Haven't I sought, in every way, to lift you up?
Haven't I?

ENGSTRAND

I don't know how as I 'd have got by if it weren't for
you, Reverend. More than once.

MANDERS

And this is the way you repay me? You have caused
me to make false entries in the parish register. You
have withheld information it was your duty as a
Christian and a citizen to reveal. You have been false.
You have been deceitful. You have been a liar. For
years and years and years. I am finished with you!

ENGSTRAND

(Sighs) Well, that's it, I suppose.

MANDERS

Oh, yes ... oh yes. You can't justify any of this. Oh no.
You are found out.

ENGSTRAND

What could I do? Let the poor girl go round telling
everybody? Bad enough what happened, without
more shame on top of it. Put yourself in her shoes,
Pastor ...

MANDERS

I?

ENGSTRAND

Well, no. Not literally. But suppose you had something that you were ashamed of ... I don't think it's up to us men to be too hard on women, sir, seeing as how they're placed.

MANDERS

I am not blaming your wife. It's you I'm talking to.

ENGSTRAND

If I could just ask your Reverence one question ...

MANDERS

Very well, go on.

ENGSTRAND

Isn't it right to try and raise up the fallen?

MANDERS

Yes!

ENGSTRAND

And isn't a man obliged to keep his word, as a matter of honour?

MANDERS

Certainly. But ...

ENGSTRAND

At the time, Johanna had her trouble with whoever it was ... the Russian, Englishman, American it could've been ... she'd already turned me down. Twice. She liked a decent-looking man, and I had this leg from trying to talk to seamen in a tavern. When I begged them to leave off the liquor ... and well, as you know, sir, they threw me down the stairs.

MRS ALVING

(*By the window*) Hmmm.

MANDERS

I know that, Engstrand. Your disability is a credit to you.

ENGSTRAND

Not that I pride myself on it, sir. Oh no. But what I wanted to say was ... when she came to me, tears all down her face, threatening something desperate. Well, it tore the heart out of me, and that's the truth.

MANDERS

Well?

ENGSTRAND

I said to her ... listen to me, Johanna. That Yankee's off, away over the seas. You won't see him again. You're here, and I'm here, and you've had a fall. And here I am on two stout legs. I meant it as a manner of speaking, sir ...

MANDERS

I understand. Go on.

ENGSTRAND

Sir, I raised her up. I gave her my hand, and the protection of my name, so's nobody could point the finger at her for carrying on and cavorting with foreigners.

MANDERS

All that was very commendable. What I cannot approve is that you accepted money.

ENGSTRAND

Money, sir? Me, sir? Not a penny.

MANDERS looks across at MRS ALVING.

ENGSTRAND

Oh yes … there was. I do remember. Johanna did have a little sum. No, I told her, no! That's the wages of sin, that is. We'll have none of it. We'll throw it back in his face. Gold, greasy banknotes, whatever they was. But he'd gone by then, you see, Pastor. Off over the ocean.

MANDERS

(*Glancing towards MRS ALVING*) I see.

ENGSTRAND

We'll put the money, I said, for the child. For its upbringing. And that's what we did, sir. I can account for every penny.

MANDERS

I see. Well, that changes things. Considerably.

ENGSTRAND

I hope and pray I've been a decent father to Regine sir. God knows I've tried, so far as it's been in my power. We're all frail, sinful mortals, and that's the truth.

MANDERS

Yes, yes, Engstrand.

ENGSTRAND

I brought up that child, and gave her, and my dear wife, a home, just like the scriptures tell us. But I never could have brought myself to come to Pastor Manders with a story of what a good deed I done in this world. No, Jakob Engstrand, keeps that to hisself. When I come to see my Pastor it's to confess my sins

and the error of my ways. Like I said, my conscience
troubles me as much as the next man's.

MANDERS

Jakob Engstrand, give me your hand.

ENGSTRAND

Oh, sir ...

MANDERS

No fuss now. (*He grasps ENGSTRAND's hand.*) There.

ENGSTRAND

If I can dare to beg the Pastor's pardon, in all
humility ...

MANDERS

No! On the contrary. I should beg your pardon.

ENGSTRAND

Oh no. No, no!

MANDERS

Yes, most definitely, yes. And I do, with all my heart.
I'm ashamed to have misjudged you. If there were a
way to show my sincere regret for doubting your good
heart. I'd like to make recompense.

ENGSTRAND

You would, Pastor?

MANDERS

I would, indeed.

ENGSTRAND

There is something that comes to mind. As you know,
with honest work, I've managed to put something
aside. And I'd like to set up a seamen's home.

MRS ALVING

You, Engstrand? You want to …

ENGSTRAND

Yes, sir. I want to create a refuge for young men …
(To MRS ALVING) … orphans of the ocean as you
might say, Ma'am. Oh, when you think of it. The
temptations that can face a young'un when he comes
ashore. But under my roof he'd be, as it were, under a
father's guidance.

MANDERS

What do you think, Mrs Alving?

ENGSTRAND

I've little enough to set it up with, God knows. But
with a kindly helping hand …

MANDERS

Mrs Alving?

She does not reply.

MANDERS

Yes. Yes. Your plan appeals to me. I shall give it some
thought. However – for now – the prayers. Go down
and light a few candles for a touch of ceremony. I
shall be very pleased to attend. We'll pray together,
Engstrand. Is everything ready?

ENGSTRAND

Oh yes, sir! And with you there … (He turns.)
Goodbye, Mrs Alving. Look after my little girl for me.
My poor Johanna's daughter. That child is part of my
own heart, I can't deny it.

ENGSTRAD bows his head to them and goes.

ACT TWO

MANDERS

Well! What do you think now, Mrs Alving? A different sort of picture, wouldn't you say?

MRS ALVING

Very much so.

MANDERS

And you see how careful we must be in judging our fellow men. How easy it is to fall into error. Well, what do you say?

MRS ALVING

What do I say? I say you have always been and always will be a big baby, Manders.

MANDERS

Me?

MRS ALVING

(Her hands on his shoulders) And it's all I can do not to wrap you up in a great big hug.

MANDERS

(Pulling away) Goodness me! No, please!

MRS ALVING

(Smiling) I didn't mean to frighten you!

MANDERS

It's just the way you express yourself sometimes. I'll … ah. (He gathers his documents, and puts them in his bag.) I'll say goodbye for the moment. You'll, ah, keep an eye on your son. I shall look in later.

MANDERS exits.

MRS ALVING sighs, and looks out of the window. She tidies the table, goes to the dining room, and stops short at the door.

MRS ALVING

Osvald! I didn't know you were there.

OSVALD

(*From the dining room*) I'm just finishing my cigar.

MRS ALVING

I thought you'd gone out.

OSVALD

In this weather?

The sound of glass and decanter.

MRS ALVING, leaving the dining room door open, settles down with her knitting by the window.

OSVALD

(*Off*) Was that the Pastor leaving?

MRS ALVING

Yes. He's gone down to the orphanage.

Again, the sound of glass and decanter.

MRS ALVING

Osvald, do take it steadily. That's very strong liquor.

OSVALD

(*Off*) It keeps out the damp.

MRS ALVING

Come in here with me.

OSVALD

(*Off*) I'm smoking.

MRS ALVING

Oh, I don't mind a cigar, you know that.

OSVALD

(*Off*) I'll just top up.

OSVALD enters, with glass and cigar.

OSVALD

Where did he go?

MRS ALVING

The Pastor? I told you, the Orphanage.

OSVALD

Oh, that's right.

MRS ALVING

You shouldn't sit at table so long.

OSVALD

It's cosy. (*He fondles her.*) I love it. Sitting at my
mother's table in my mother's room, enjoying
delicious food.

MRS ALVING

Oh, my dear boy . . .

OSVALD

(*Gets up abruptly*) What else is there? Not as though I
can do anything.

MRS ALVING

Can't you?

OSVALD

In this? (*He gestures to the mist outside.*) No sun! Not
a glimmer, all day long! (*Paces*)

MRS ALVING

Perhaps it wasn't such a good idea to come home.

OSVALD

No. I had to.

MRS ALVING

Believe me, I'd sacrifice the joy of having you here ten times over if I thought ...

OSVALD

(*Stops by the table*) Is it such a joy? Having me back?

MRS ALVING

What a question! How can you ask that?

OSVALD

I'm surprised it matters to you whether I'm here or not.

MRS ALVING

How can you say that?

OSVALD

You've managed very well without me.

MRS ALVING

I've existed without you, that's true.

Silence. Dusk deepens.

OSVALD puts down his cigar, paces.

OSVALD

(*Stops by MRS ALVING*) May I?

She makes room for him on the sofa.

MRS ALVING

Please, dearest.

OSVALD

(*Sits*) There's something I have to tell you.

MRS ALVING

(*Nervously*) Oh?

OSVALD

Because I can't bear it any longer.

MRS ALVING

Bear what?

OSVALD

I couldn't bring myself to write, and ever since I've
been back ...

MRS ALVING

(*Grasps his arm*) Osvald, what is it?

OSVALD

All yesterday and all today I've been trying to get rid
of the thoughts in my head ... it's no good ...

MRS ALVING

(*Rises*) Tell me.

OSVALD

(*Pulls her down beside him*) Please. (*She sits*) I'll try
and ... I've said I was tired.

MRS ALVING

After the journey, yes ...

OSVALD

It's not that. It's not ordinary tiredness.

MRS ALVING

(*Tries to rise*) Osvald, are you ill?

OSVALD

(*Pulls her down again*) Sit down, Mother. Try not to
be upset. I'm not ill in the ordinary sense. (*He puts*

*his hands to his head.)* It's my mind. It's broken down.
It doesn't work anymore. I can't . . .

He throws himself into her lap, and sobs deeply.

**MRS ALVING**

*(Trembling)* Osvald. No, look at me! What's the
matter?

**OSVALD**

*(Looks up at her in despair)* I'll never work again. Can
you imagine not being able to work, Mother? It's like
being dead.

**MRS ALVING**

My darling! What happened to you?

**OSVALD**

*(Sits up)* I don't understand it. I've never led a wild
life. Not in that way.

**MRS ALVING**

Of course you haven't.

**OSVALD**

And yet I have this horrible thing!

**MRS ALVING**

No. You'll be all right. You're suffering from nervous
exhaustion. It's nothing more than that.

**OSVALD**

That's what I thought in the beginning. *(He shakes
his head.)*

**MRS ALVING**

Tell me about it. When did you first feel ill?

OSVALD

In Paris, after my last visit home. I began to have
these pains. In my head.

MRS ALVING

Paris ...

OSVALD

I've had headaches ever since I was little, so I didn't
think they were ...

MRS ALVING

Yes ... ?

OSVALD

They got worse. I couldn't work. I tried to start a
new painting, a big canvas, but I couldn't focus my
thoughts. It was as if something was paralyzing my
mind. I had no strength. Everything swam round and
round. In the end, I sent for a doctor.

MRS ALVING

And?

OSVALD

He asked me questions.

MRS ALVING

Questions? What about?

OSVALD

About everything. From when I was small. My life as
a student in Paris. My life now.

MRS ALVING

Did he know what was wrong?

Silence.

OSVALD

He told me that I was more or less finished. Eaten out from the time I was born. Vermoulu was the word he used. Worm-eaten.

MRS ALVING

(*Tensely*) What's that supposed to mean?!

OSVALD

I didn't understand. I asked him to be more specific. He said … he said …

MRS ALVING

What?

OSVALD

That the sins of the father are visited upon the children.

MRS ALVING

(*Rises slowly*) The father?

OSVALD

I almost hit him in the face!

MRS ALVING moves away across the room.

OSVALD

Can you imagine? I told him: 'That's impossible!' He still wouldn't believe me, the filthy old cynic. I had to show him your letters! I sat down with him and translated all the parts about father to prove that it was impossible. That my father was beyond reproach.

MRS ALVING

What did he say then?

OSVALD

He had to admit he was wrong. That's when I realised.
The truth. That the life I'd been living with my
friends ... that made me come alive ... was too much
for me.

He collapses, hiding his face. MRS ALVING paces in anguish.

He looks up.

OSVALD

If only it were inherited. Not my own fault! But to lose
my health, any chance of happiness ... because of
something I picked up in Paris. I should never have
gone!

MRS ALVING

No. No, dearest. It's not as bad as you think.

OSVALD

You don't know. (Jumps up) And what I've done to
you! I almost wish you didn't care for me so much.

MRS ALVING

Oh, Osvald, my lovely boy. You're all I have in the
world. You're all I've ever wanted.

OSVALD

(Kisses her hands) I know. Now that I'm here, I know.
It makes it ... We won't talk any more, not today ... I
can't bear to think of it for long. Is there something to
drink?

MRS ALVING

Now? What do you want?

OSVALD

Anything. Cold punch. Anything ...

MRS ALVING

But Osvald ...

OSVALD

Don't Mother. I must have something. Anything. I can't bear thinking!

He goes into the conservatory.

OSVALD

It's so dark in here!

MRS ALVING crosses, and pulls the bell ring.

OSVALD

This interminable rain. In all my visits home, I never once remember seeing the sun.

MRS ALVING

You're not thinking of leaving?

OSVALD

(*Sighs deeply*) I'm not thinking of anything. I can't think.

REGINE enters from dining room.

REGINE

You rang, Ma'am?

MRS ALVING

Yes. Bring in the lamp.

REGINE

Right away. I've just lit it.

REGINE exits.

MRS ALVING

Osvald. You won't keep anything from me?

OSVALD

Haven't I told you enough?

REGINE comes in with the lamp.

MRS ALVING

Oh, and Regine, bring us a half bottle of champagne.

REGINE

Yes Ma'am.

REGINE goes

OSVALD

Thank you. I knew you wouldn't refuse me.

MRS ALVING

I won't refuse you anything.

OSVALD

Do you mean that, Mother? Do you mean it? (*He holds her face.*) Do you mean that you won't refuse me anything?

MRS ALVING

Dearest...

OSVALD

Sssh.

REGINE returns with the wine on a tray.

REGINE

Shall I open it?

OSVALD

No thanks, I'll do it.

REGINE goes out.

MRS ALVING

What did you mean? What mustn't I refuse you?

OSVALD

First a glass.

He fills a glass.

MRS ALVING

Thank you, no. Not for me.

He drinks, refills his glass, and sits at the table.

MRS ALVING

Well?

OSVALD

(Without looking at her) You seemed very quiet at
lunch – you and Manders.

MRS ALVING

Oh?

OSVALD

(Silence) Tell me, what do you think of Regine, isn't
she wonderful?

MRS ALVING

Osvald, you don't know her as well as I do.

OSVALD

You must admit she's beautiful.

MRS ALVING

Regine has a great many faults. I should have brought
her into the house sooner.

OSVALD

What does that matter? (He drinks.)

MRS ALVING

At all events, I'm responsible for her. I wouldn't want
her to be hurt.

OSVALD

(*Jumps up*) But can't you see? You must see, she's my
only hope!

MRS ALVING

(*Rising*) What do you mean?

OSVALD

I can't bear to be on my own.

MRS ALVING

You have me.

OSVALD

Yes. That's why I came home. But it won't work. I can't
live here.

MRS ALVING

Osvald!

OSVALD

I have to live my own way. I must go in any case. I
don't want you to see it.

MRS ALVING

But if you're ill ...

OSVALD

If it were just the illness, I'd stay. (*Pacing restlessly*)
Can't you see, it's all the rest! Waste. Remorse.
Feeling so ... And I'm afraid. I'm frightened.

MRS ALVING

Darling, why?

OSVALD

I don't know. I can't talk about it.

MRS ALVING crosses and rings the bell.

OSVALD

What are you doing?

MRS ALVING

Making you happy. I won't have you like this.

REGINE enters

REGINE

Yes, Ma'am?

MRS ALVING

More champagne, Regine. A big bottle.

REGINE exits.

MRS ALVING

You see? We know how to live here!

OSVALD

She's magnificent. So healthy!

MRS ALVING

Osvald, sit down. I have to talk to you.

OSVALD

(Sits) There's something I must put right, with
Regine.

MRS ALVING

Not now.

OSVALD

It's just a little thing. Quite innocent really. It was
when I was home last time. She kept asking me about
Paris.

MRS ALVING

Paris?

OSVALD

She went on and on. It was exciting for her. I asked
her if she'd like to go, and she blushed. I don't know
why I said it. Anyway, I asked her.

MRS ALVING

To go to Paris?

OSVALD

I forgot all about it! Yesterday, when I asked her
if she was pleased I was back, she reminded me.
She thought I'd meant it. She'd even been learning
French!

MRS ALVING

Osvald, no.

OSVALD

Isn't she splendid? I'd never really noticed before. All
that shining warmth and vitality. Beauty. And it was
as if her arms were open, ready to embrace me.

MRS ALVING

Oh, my dear.

OSVALD

I saw salvation, Mother. She has the joy of life in her!

REGINE enters with the champagne.

REGINE

I had to go down to the cellar.

OSVALD

Get another glass, Regine. One for yourself.

REGINE

Me? *(She looks to MRS ALVING.)*

MRS ALVING

Yes, get it, Regine.

REGINE goes.

OSVALD

Look at the way she walks. So confident ...

MRS ALVING

Osvald, this mustn't happen.

OSVALD

Don't say anymore. It's settled.

REGINE returns with the glass.

OSVALD

Sit down, Regine. You see, Mother, I never find any joy here. It's to do with the joy of working. But no- one believes in that here. Here work's a punishment. Something to be endured. Life is a burden, a pain to be suffered. Something to be out of as soon as we can.

MRS ALVING

A vale of tears. We certainly do our best to make it so.

OSVALD

But down there they don't believe that. No-one thinks like that. To be alive is a miracle. A blissful experience! Haven't you seen it in my paintings? Everything I've painted is full of light! Sun. The sun. people radiant with joy. Pleasure. I can't come back here. It will kill me.

MRS ALVING rises.

**MRS ALVING**

Osvald, I must speak to you.

**REGINE**

Shall I go?

**MRS ALVING**

No, stay Regine. I must tell you everything. Both of you.

**OSVALD**

Manders is coming back ...

MANDERS enters.

**MANDERS**

We've had truly heat-warming prayers. Engstrand is a fine man. He is going to need some help with his Home for Seamen, and Regine should move back with him.

**REGINE**

No, thanks!

**MANDERS**

(*Notices her*) What are you doing here, girl? And with a glass in your hand!

**REGINE**

(*Puts it down quickly*) Beg your pardon, Mr Manders.

**OSVALD**

Regine will be coming away with me, Pastor.

**MANDERS**

What?!

**OSVALD**

As my wife, if she will agree to it.

MANDERS

Dear God in Heaven!

REGINE

It weren't me, Mr Manders.

OSVALD

Or, if I stay, she'll stay.

MANDERS

Mrs Alving, is this true?

MRS ALVING

It won't happen, any of it.

OSVALD

Why not?

MRS ALVING

Because I shall tell you the truth.

MANDERS

No, no, Mrs Alving! You can't do that.

MRS ALVING

Yes, I can. And without harming anyone.

OSVALD

Mother, what is it?

REGINE

(Listens) Mrs Alving – listen! What are they shouting
for? (She goes to the conservatory and looks out.)

OSVALD

(Moves to the window) What is that light in the sky?

REGINE

It's the orphanage! It's burning!

MRS ALVING hurries to the window.

MRS ALVING

Burning?

MANDERS

No, no, impossible. I've just come back from there!

OSVALD

No! Not my father's Refuge!

OSVALD rushes out through the garden door.

MRS ALVING

My shawl, Regine - quickly!

MANDERS

No! Oh, this is dreadful!

MRS ALVING

Come, Regine ...

MRS ALVING and REGINE go quickly.

MANDERS

(*His voice trembling*) And no insurance! We're not
insured!

He follows them out.

*Fade to black.*

# ACT THREE

The same room, with the doors open.

The lamp, alight, is on the table. Through the window, can be seen a dark red glow in the distance.

MRS ALVING, her head draped in a large shawl, stands in the conservatory, gazing.

REGINE, a shawl about her shoulders, stands behind her.

> **MRS ALVING**
>
> It's finished. Burnt to the ground.

> **REGINE**
>
> The basement's still alight!

> **MRS ALVING**
>
> Why doesn't he come in? There's nothing left to save!

> **REGINE**
>
> Shall I take him his coat?

> **MRS ALVING**
>
> No, I'll go and find him.

MRS ALVING takes the coat, and exits into the garden.

MANDERS enters separately.

> **MANDERS**
>
> Where is she? Where's Mrs Alving?

> **REGINE**
>
> In the garden.

> **MANDERS**
>
> What a dreadful night!

# ACT THREE

REGINE

It's awful, Pastor. How could it have happened?

MANDERS shakes his head.

ENGSTRAND enters.

ENGSTRAND

Pastor ...

MANDERS

Stop following me, man!

ENGSTRAND

God help me, sir, but I have to! Lord help us, but this is
a terrible mess, Pastor.

MANDERS

Be quiet.

REGINE

Mess?

ENGSTRAND

It was on account of the prayer meeting. (*Sotto voce*)
We've caught the old devil now, girl. (*Aloud*) And to
think it was my fault that it's Pastor Manders' fault!

MANDERS

My fault? Engstrand, I ...

ENGSTRAND

But it was you, sir! Nobody but you was messing about
with those candles.

MANDERS

So you keep saying. So you keep saying. But I don't
remember having a candle in my hand.

ENGSTRAND

I saw you, sir. The Pastor took the candle like this ...
and pinched it out with his fingers, like this. And
flicked the tip of the wick down – like this. Down
among the shavings.

MANDERS

You saw me do that?

ENGSTRAND

As plain as day.

MANDERS

I don't understand. I don't do that. I never snuff
candles with my fingers.

MANDERS walks restlessly.

ENGSTRAND

(Keeping pace with him.) And, your Reverence,
without insurance. You hadn't insured the place, had
you? (To REGINE) No insurance.

MANDERS swerves but ENGSTRAND dogs him.

ENGSTRAND

No insurance. And then to go over and set the place
on fire. God help us. What a terrible misfortune.

MANDERS

It is. It is indeed.

ENGSTRAND

And to happen to a charitable institution set up to
serve all the community. Oh, Pastor, think of the
newspapers! Oh, they'll come down hard on you, they
will.

MANDERS

D'you think I don't know that? I can't bear to think
about it.

MRS ALVING enters.

MRS ALVING

Osvald is standing over the embers. I can't get him to
move.

MANDERS

There you are, Mrs Alving!

MRS ALVING

Ah, Pastor! So, you got out of making your speech?

MANDERS

Not at all. The occasion should have been a glorious
one, but the Lord has decreed otherwise. We bow to
His will.

MRS ALVING

(*Low*) I'm not sorry it's happened.

MANDERS

Not sorry? How can you say such a thing?

MRS ALVING

The reasons for the orphanage were not as they
should have been, don't you think so?

MANDERS

Nonetheless ...

MRS ALVING

Don't you?

MANDERS

Nonetheless, it's a tragedy.

**MRS ALVING**

We need to discuss the business implications.
Engstrand, did you want something?

**ENGSTRAND**

I was waiting for the Pastor.

**MRS ALVING**

Then do sit down.

**ENGSTRAND**

That's all right. I can stand.

**MRS ALVING**

(*To MANDERS*) You'll be leaving by the steamer
tonight?

**MANDERS**

Yes, in just over an hour's time.

**MRS ALVING**

I want no more of all this. Take the papers with you
and decide what is to be done. I've other things to
think about.

**MANDERS**

Mrs Alving . . .

**MRS ALVING**

I shall be sending you power of attorney. Settle
everything as you see fit.

**MANDERS**

Are you sure? You realize that the terms of the
original bequest will need to be completely altered?

**MRS ALVING**

Then do it.

MANDERS

We could make the property over to the parish. The land could most certainly be put to use. Then there's the interest on the money in the bank, which could be used to benefit some charity in the town.

MRS ALVING

Whatever you say. It's all the same to me.

ENGSTRAND

There is the seaman's home, sir.

MANDER

Oh yes, that's a possibility. Of course it will have to be gone into.

ENGSTRAND

(Sotto voce) Oh, will it? To hell with that.

MANDERS

(Sighs) And there is, of course, the question: will I be able to undertake these obligations? Public opinion may force me to withdraw. It all depends on the results of the official enquiry.

MRS ALVING

How do you mean?

MANDERS

Who knows what the results will be?

MRS ALVING

(Puzzled) I'm sorry? Results? There has been an accident. A fire. An accident.

MANDERS

That's as may be. There will still be those who seek to cast blame. The enquiry may decide that I, as the senior adviser, have failed in my responsibility.

ENGSTRAND

Never. (*He sidles up to MANDERS.*) Not with old Engstrand here at your side. (*Lowers his voice.*) Engstrand's not the man to desert a worthy benefactor in his hour of need, so to speak.

MANDERS

But my dear man, you ...

ENGSTRAND

Jakob Engstrand will be your guardian angel. Let him take the burden.

MANDERS

Oh no. No, no, no. That I couldn't allow.

ENGSTRAND

It's how it's going to be. To protect a fine man who's irreplaceable. Let a poor sinner step forward. Lord knows it won't be the first time he's taken the blame for another.

MANDERS

(*Grabs ENGSTRAND's hand*) Jakob! You are that rare man – a true Christian! Take my word, you shall have all the help you need to establish your Seaman's Refuge. Count on me.

ENGSTRAND makes to reply, but seems overcome by feeling.

MANDERS puts his pack over his shoulder, and takes MRS ALVING'S hands.

MANDERS

I must make my farewells. God be with you. (*To
ENGSTRAND*) We'll journey together.

ENGSTRAND

(*At the dining room door*) Regine! Come on, girl. Get
yourself ready! (*Lower*) There's a life in town for you
softer than a duck's nest, take my word!

REGINE

Oh, merci, I'm sure. Not likely! (*Fetching MANDERS'
coat and umbrella.*)

ENGSTRAND

You'll be snugger than a yolk in a pullet's egg.

REGINE

Let go!

They tussle. She swipes at him and pulls away.

MANDERS

Goodbye to you, Mrs Alving. May peace and order
soon dwell again under this roof.

MRS ALVING

Goodbye.

MRS ALVING turns quickly, and goes into the conservatory as
OSVALD arrives, wet from being splashed by the hoses.

ENGSTRAND and REGINE help MANDERS into his coat, muttering
to each other behind his back. REGINE spits in his face.

ENGSTRAND

(*Genial in front of MANDERS*) Well, goodbye, girl.
If you're ever in any trouble, you know where to
find me. (*Low*) Little Harbour Street, all right? (*To
MRS ALVING and OSVALD*) I thought you'd like

to know. The name of my home for seafaring men will be 'Captain Alving's Home for Seamen.' If the opportunity to run this house as I would wish is afforded me, then I promise you that it will be worthy of his great and beloved name. God bless the Captain.

MANDERS
(*At the door*) Yes, yes. Come along, Engstrand. Goodbye! Goodbye!

MANDERS and ENGSTRAND go.

OSVALD
What did he mean? What house?

MRS ALVING
A sort of home. He wants to set up a refuge, with the Pastor.

OSVALD
It'll burn, the same as this.

MRS ALVING
Why do you say that?

OSVALD
It'll all burn. There'll be nothing left in father's memory. I'm burning.

REGINE stares at him, perturbed.

MRS ALVING
Osvald! My dear, you shouldn't have stayed out there all this time.

OSVALD sits at the table.

MRS ALVING
Let me dry your face, you're dripping wet!

OSVALD gazes into space.

MRS ALVING

Are you tired? Perhaps you should go to bed and get
some sleep.

OSVALD

Sleep? Sleep … *(Dully)* I'll sleep soon enough.

REGINE

Is Mr Alving ill?

OSVALD

Shut the doors!

MRS ALVING

Shut the doors, Regine.

REGINE shuts the doors, and remains standing.

MRS ALVING takes off her shawl. REGINE does likewise.

MRS ALVING

*(Sits by OSVALD)* I'll sit with you.

OSVALD

Please. Regine must stay here too. I want her close to
me all the time. You'll help me, won't you, Regine?

REGINE

Sorry?

OSVALD

*(To REGINE)* When I need it.

MRS ALVING

Osvald, I'm here.

OSVALD

You? *(Smiling)* No, Mother, you wouldn't help me with this. *(With a sad laugh)* Ha ... No, not you. It should be you, Regine ...

REGINE

Yes, Mr Alving?

OSVALD

Look at me. Why is she so awkward? Can't you call me by my Christian name?

REGINE

I don't think Mrs Alving would like it.

MRS ALVING

You may have every right to soon Regine. Please, come and sit down with us.

After a moment, REGINE sits shyly across the table.

MRS ALVING

And now, my poor troubled boy, I'm going to take this burden from you ...

OSVALD

You?

MRS ALVING

... all the remorse, all the self-reproach you've been suffering.

OSVALD

You think you can do that?!

MRS ALVING

Ssh! *(She walks.)* Earlier on, when you were speaking of the joy of life, a door opened. Suddenly I saw the

whole of my life, everything that's happened, in a new
way. It was as if the room suddenly filled with light.

OSVALD

What are you talking about?

MRS ALVING

I wish you could have known your father when he was
a young lieutenant. He had such joy – so much life.

OSVALD

I know.

MRS ALVING

It was like a feast day just to stand and look at him.
All that strength – energy.

She goes silent.

OSVALD

I remember.

MRS ALVING

But then you see, this child of joy, this free spirit,
was persuaded to make a life inside a dead world.
In a small town with nothing to do. Nothing to
amaze, intrigue, challenge the mind. Nothing to
inspire, provide purpose. Not a friend of quality,
not one colleague with dimension, imagination,
understanding. Nothing, no-one to engage him heart
and soul. Just a social position to maintain. And
distractions.

OSVALD

Distractions? What are you saying?

MRS ALVING

There was no way of life for him. Nothing to satisfy
that beautiful, dancing energy.

OSVALD

He had you.

MRS ALVING

(*Flat*) Yes. He had me. His well-brought-up wife. So
drilled and trained in the idea of duty. His duty. My
duty. So steeped in notions of life as a long, bare
road of stoical endurance that I made this house
unbearable for him. He sought respite. He went where
there was light and warmth, and what seemed to be a
welcome.

OSVALD

You've never told me this.

MRS ALVING

You're his son. You love him.

OSVALD

Why are you telling me now?

MRS ALVING

(*Slowly*) Because . . . because I've always known that
your father was damaged. Before you were born.

OSVALD

(*Cries out*) Ahhh!

He leaps to his feet, and goes to the window.

MRS ALVING

And I knew . . . as well . . . that Regine has as much
right to be under this roof as my own son.

OSVALD

(*Turns*) Regine?

REGINE

(*Jumps up*) Me?

MRS ALVING

As her birthright.

OSVALD

Regine?!

REGINE

What's all this? What are you saying?

MRS ALVING

Your mother was not at fault, Regine. She was a
decent woman,

REGINE

Decent? It doesn't sound like it. Not if what you're
saying is true, that I'm ... I have wondered. The way
you've always looked out for me. I thought it was
'cause you liked me. I can't stay here, Madam. I can't.
I'll have to leave right away.

MRS ALVING

Is that what you really want?

REGINE

Yes!!

MRS ALVING

You can do as you wish, naturally.

REGINE

Does Pastor Manders know about this?

MRS ALVING

Yes, he knows about it.

REGINE

(*Putting on her shawl*) Then I'd better see if I can catch him. I always get on with the Pastor. I've as much right to the money as that filthy old carpenter.

MRS ALVING

As for money, let me help you with that.

REGINE

(*Looks at her sharply*) Bit late now. You could have raised me as a gentleman's daughter, but you didn't. Oh, what the hell! (*She glances at the bottle of champagne.*) Don't you worry, I'll get my glass of champagne out of life. You see if I don't.

MRS ALVING

If you ever need a home, you know where to find me.

REGINE

No, thanks. Paster Manders will look after me. If he doesn't, I'm set up in Captain Alving's Refuge. Plenty of pickings there!

MRS ALVING

Regine, no! You'll be ruined!

REGINE

Who cares? Adieu to the pair of you!

REGINE curtsies and goes.

OSVALD

(*Looking out of the window.*) Has she gone?

MRS ALVING

Yes.

OSVALD

It's insane. All of it.

MRS ALVING

(*Puts her hands on his shoulders.*) Has it upset you?

OSVALD

About Father, you mean?

MRS ALVING

It's been a shock. I can see that.

OSVALD

No, it's not. I'm surprised, but what difference does it make?

MRS ALVING

(*Stands back*) You don't mind? That your father was so – unhappy?

OSVALD

I feel sympathy … as you would for anyone.

MRS ALVING

But nothing more? For your own father?

OSVALD

Father? I never knew him! All I remember is him making me smoke that cigar and being sick all over the floor.

MRS ALVING

That's awful. But you <u>are</u> his child.

OSVALD

I don't know him. I never did. 'The child should love the parent?' Don't tell me you believe that? You're usually so enlightened. (*Turns to her*) It's just a superstition. An idea. It has no substance.

MRS ALVING

Like a ghost, you mean? (*She shudders.*)

OSVALD

If you like.

MRS ALVING

Then Osvald, you don't love me either!

OSVALD

At least I know you.

MRS ALVING

Is that all?

OSVALD

I know you care about me. I'm grateful for that. It's useful now that I'm ill.

MRS ALVING

It is, isn't it? Oh, I'm almost glad you're ill. That you had to come home. You're not really mine yet. I still have to win you.

OSVALD

(*Impatient*) Yes, yes, well, if you want to think of it that way. I'm ill, Mother. I can't be concerned with ... There's enough, just thinking about myself.

MRS ALVING

Don't worry, I'll take care of you. I'll be a good nurse, I'll be quiet and patient.

OSVALD

And cheerful, I hope?

MRS ALVING

You're right. Now tell me, have I taken away all that dreadful remorse and self-hatred and pain?

OSVALD

I'm still afraid. Regine could have taken away the fright.

MRS ALVING

How?

OSVALD

Is it very late, Mother?

MRS ALVING

Nearly morning. (*Looks out through the conservatory*) There's the first light of dawn on the mountains. It's going to be a fine day, Osvald. You'll see the sun soon.

OSVALD

Good. Oh, there's still so much to live for!

MRS ALVING

Of course, there is.

OSVALD

Even if I can't work, I ...

MRS ALVING

Oh, my dearest but you will. You'll work again. Now that you're rid of all the anxiety and awful thoughts.

OSVALD

Yes. Thank you for that. There at least I'm free. (*He sits down on the sofa.*) Mother, I have to talk to you.

MRS ALVING

(*Pushes an armchair close to him.*) Dearest?

OSVALD

By the time the sun is up you'll know everything. Perhaps then I shan't be afraid.

MRS ALVING

Know what, dearest?

OSVALD

You mustn't scream, or shriek. Promise me you won't shriek. We'll sit here quietly together, and we'll simply talk. Promise me?

MRS ALVING

I promise. But what is it?

OSVALD

You've got to understand. All this talk of tiredness … not being able to work … those are just the symptoms.

MRS ALVING

Of what?

OSVALD

Of the illness.

MRS ALVING

What illness?

OSVALD

The illness I inherited. *(Points to his head.)* Here. It's sitting – in here – waiting. It can attack at any time.

MRS ALVING

But that's horrible.

OSVALD

Please. Don't get excited. Now you know how it is.

MRS ALVING

*(Jumps up)* No, it's not true, Osvald. It can't be.

OSVALD

I've already had one attack. But then it went away.
All that's left is the fright and that never goes. That's
why had to come home.

MRS ALVING

Because you were afraid.

OSVALD

Yes. Because it's so disgusting. That's the unbearable
part of it. I could bear some ordinary disease, even
if I knew it was going to kill me. I'm not so afraid of
dying. It's the thought being helpless. Dribbling like a
child. Having to be fed. Lying in my own ...

MRS ALVING

I'm here, darling. I'm here to nurse you.

OSVALD

(Jumps up) The thought of it – lying in wait for years.
Suppose you die first? It might not kill me at once, the
doctor said. There could be a sort of ... softening of
the brain. (Smiles) What a lovely expression. Makes
you think of velvet curtains.

MRS ALVING

Osvald!

OSVALD

(He paces the floor) If I had Regine, she'd do it. She'd
help me.

MRS ALVING

(Goes to him) I'll help you. You know I will.

OSVALD

After I recovered, he told me that the next time might
be ... it might be the end for me.

MRS ALVING

That's heartless. How could he say that?

OSVALD

I made him tell me. I said I had to make
arrangements.

He takes out a small box, and shows his mother.

MRS ALVING

What ... what is it?

OSVALD

Morphine. I've managed to collect twelve ampules.

MRS ALVING

Give it to me!

OSVALD

Not yet. (*Puts the box back in his pocket.*) If Regine
were here, she'd do it for me. I know she would. She'd
do me this one last favour.

MRS ALVING

No! Never!

OSVALD

If she saw me lying there helpless. Drooling.

MRS ALVING

No she wouldn't!

OSVALD

Oh yes, she would. Regine's full of life! She wouldn't
put up with nursing a drooling idiot – not Regine.

MRS ALVING

Then I thank the Lord she's not here.

OSVALD

So, d'you see? That leaves you.

MRS ALVING

No. I won't do it. I couldn't.

OSVALD

Who else?

MRS ALVING

But I'm your mother! I gave you life.

OSVALD

I never asked you for it. I don't want it. Take it back!

MRS ALVING

Oh, God help me. Help me!

MRS ALVING runs out into the hall.

OSVALD

Where are you going? Don't leave me!

OSVALD follows her.

MRS ALVING

(In the hall) To fetch the Doctor. No, let me!

OSVALD

(In the hall) Don't leave. (He locks the front door) I . . .
I don't want anyone here.

MRS ALVING

(Comes into the room) Osvald. Osvald, my dear . . . Oh,
my son . . .

OSVALD

(Follows her back from the hall) Don't you love me?
Don't you care that I feel this way? That I'm afraid?

MRS ALVING

(*Masters her feelings.*) You know I do. (*She gives him her hand.*)

OSVALD

Then you promise?

MRS ALVING

If ever it's necessary. But it won't be necessary. I don't believe it. Because it's impossible.

OSVALD

Well, we can hope so. In the meantime, we'll live together for as long as we can. Thank you, Mother.

He settles in the armchair. Dawn is breaking.

MRS ALVING

Do you feel better now?

OSVALD

Yes.

MRS ALVING

(*Bends over him.*) It's all been a terrible nightmare. But you're home now. You can rest here now, at home with your own mother. Anything you want is yours. Just as it was when you were little. There. You see? All over. No more pain. You see how quickly it went away? I knew it would.

As the sun rises, glaciers and peaks shine brilliantly in the distance. OSVALD sits motionless, facing downstage, away from the view.

MRS ALVING

Osvald – the sun! We're going to have a lovely day! Look, now you can really see your home!

She crosses to the table and puts out the lamp.

OSVALD

(*Abruptly*) Mother, give me the sun.

MRS ALVING, by the table, turns to him, startled.

MRS ALVING

What did you say?

OSVALD

(*Repeats in a dull monotone*) The sun. The sun.

MRS ALVING moves across to him.

MRS ALVING

Osvald, what's the matter?

OSVALD shrinks in the chair. He slumps. There is no expression in his face. His eyes stare ahead without seeing.

MRS ALVING

(*Very frightened*) What is it? (*She screams*) Osvald! What's wrong with you?

She drops on her knees by his side, and starts to shake him.

MRS ALVING

Osvald! Osvald, look at me. Look at me!

OSVALD

(*In the same, dull voice*) The sun – the sun.

MRS ALVING

Don't you know me?

MRS ALVING jumps up in agony, tearing at her hair.

MRS ALVING

(*Screams*) No! I can't bear this ... I can't bear this ... !

Her voice drops to a whisper.

MRS ALVING

I can't bear this. No ... Where is ...?

She searches his pockets for the morphine.

MRS ALVING

Ah!

She finds the box, but steps back in horror.

MRS ALVING

(*Screams*) No, no! Yes ... no, no ... no!

She stands back from him, tearing at her hair, and shuddering in horror.

OSVALD

The sun. The sun.

*Fade to black.*

The End

# HEDDA GABLER

by Henrik Ibsen

in a version by Pam Gems

for Nancy Meckler

# HEDDA GABLER

## Characters

Hedda Gabler (now Hedda Tesman)

Jorgen Tesman

Miss Tesman (Aunt Julla)

Berta

Judge Brack

Thea Elvsted

Eilert Lvborg

# HEDDA GABLER

## ACT ONE

Morning sunlight.

A handsome Drawing Room decorated with several vases of flowers.

Upstage is a curtained inner room. A sofa, table and chairs are visible in the inner room, which is dominated by the commanding portrait of a General in uniform.

Stage right: the hall.

Stage left: French windows with gardens beyond.

Downstage: a table and chairs. Down right: a porcelain stove, an armchair and two footstools. Down Left: another sofa.

Upstage right: a sofa and table. Up Left: a piano.

MISS TESMAN enters from the hall followed by BERTA, who is carrying wrapped flowers.

MISS TESMAN is in her sixties, BERTA somewhat older.

                    MISS TESMAN
        Still in bed?

                    BERTA
        Still in bed.

They savour this for a moment.

                    MISS TESMAN
        (*A return to propriety*) It <u>was</u> after midnight when
        they arrived.

BERTA

And when they did come in, all the luggage had to be
unpacked – right then and there!

MISS TESMAN

Not everything, surely?

BERTA

Every single blessed thing. And put away properly.
She wouldn't go up till we done it all, Miss Julla.

MISS TESMAN

Well, we mustn't disturb them.

She crosses, draws back the curtains, and opens the French
windows.

MISS TESMAN

That's better.

BERTA unwraps the flowers, brings a vase, fills it from an
enamelled can, and looks round, holding the flowers.

BERTA

I don't know where I'm going to put these. There's no
room.

MISS TESMAN makes a space, and watches BERTA tweak the new
arrangement to their mutual satisfaction.

BERTA

There.

They regard the flowers fondly, and look at each other.

MISS TESMAN

Well, Berta.

BERTA

Well, Miss Julla.

MISS TESMAN

(*Looking around*) A big change for us all.

BERTA

That's true enough.

MISS TESMAN

Don't think it's been easy, losing you after all these years ...

BERTA

... all these years ...

MISS TESMAN

But what else could we do? You've looked after him since he was in swaddling clothes.

BERTA

(*Nods agreement*) ... clothes. It's Miss Rina worries me, Miss Ju. That new girl'll never manage. What do she know about invalids?

MISS TESMAN

Now Berta you're not to worry. Yours truly will take the brunt of it. I'll look after Rina. We'll manage somehow.

BERTA

Anyway, I might not suit here. She's got her own way of doing things.

MISS TESMAN

We must both live and learn. Hedda's bound to be particular.

BERTA

That's the trouble. I've never worked for a lady before.

MISS TESMAN

General Gabler's daughter!

BERTA

. . . daughter. I know!

MISS TESMAN

Riding out with her father.

BERTA

. . . her father, all in black . . .

MISS TESMAN

With the long skirt.

BERTA

And the feather in her hat. (*Shakes her head*) Who'd
have dreamt of a match between her and our little
Jorgie with all his books and his papers.

MISS TESMAN

A dream come true. By the way, Berta, remember not
to call him little Jorgie or Master Jorgen any more.

BERTA

Ooh yes, I'm sorry.

MISS TESMAN

You must say Doctor, then his surname. Doctor
Tesman.

BERTA

Doctor Tesman. She put me right last night, as soon
as they come through the door. It's true then, Miss?

MISS TESMAN

Oh yes. Jorgie whispered in my ear the minute he saw
me. Some foreign university has made him a doctor.
Our Jorgie, a doctor!

#### BERTA

I'm not surprised. That boy's brains, he could be anything. Mind you, I never thought he'd go in for cutting people up.

#### MISS TESMAN

Oh no, it's not that sort of doctor, Berta. You can be a doctor of anything.

#### BERTA

*(Baffled)* Anything?

#### MISS TESMAN

Oh yes. What is more, what is more – you may have to call him something even more elevated soon. Something even more important.

#### BERTA

Never! What?

#### MISS TESMAN

*(Smiles)* Ah, that would be telling. Oh, dear Lord . . . if only our poor Jochum could have been spared to see what's become of his little boy. *(She looks around suddenly)* Berta! What's happened to the covers?

#### BERTA

I had to take them off last night and put them away. She doesn't like loose covers.

#### MISS TESMAN

Surely, they're not going to use this room every day?

BERTA shrugs

#### MISS TESMAN

What does Jorgie say?

BERTA

Never opened his mouth.

JORGEN TESMAN enters. He is in his 30s, a comfortable, amiable man in glasses.

MISS TESMAN

Good morning!

JORGEN

Aunt Julla! What are you doing here? I thought you'd still be in bed after waiting up half the night for us!

MISS TESMAN

I just came over to make sure you were settled in.

JORGEN

You can't have had more than a wink of sleep.

MISS TESMAN

Oh, it won't hurt me to lose a night's rest.

JORGEN

You got home safely?

MISS TESMAN

Judge Brack saw me all the way to my front door, bless him.

JORGEN

I'm so sorry we couldn't fit you in the carriage ... with all Hedda's things.

MISS TESMAN

I've never seen so much luggage in all my life!

BERTA

(*Whispers in his ear*) Shall I go up, Jorg ... Mister ... Doctor? In case Madam needs anything?

JORGEN

Better not disturb her. She'll ring when she wants
you.

Absently, he hands her a BAG so heavy that she keels over.

JORGEN

Just some books to go up to the attic.

She struggles off.

MISS TESMAN

Oh Jorgie, laden as usual. You and those old books!

JORGEN

Not books, Aunt, treasure! Booty! There isn't an
archive in the whole of Europe that hasn't been
traced, unearthed and mined. By me. I have twenty
notebooks of references that I swear to you, Aunt,
have never been disinterred before, ever.

MISS TESMAN

Oh, lovely. You didn't spend all your time
honeymooning, then?

JORGEN

Of course not. You've no idea what I've uncovered. I
can't wait to get ... but, dearest Aunt, never mind me.
Welcome to my new abode! Sit down. Make yourself
at home!

He leans over her fondly, and unties her bonnet. She takes it off
and hands it to him.

MISS TESMAN

Bless you.

JORGEN

This is a very fine hat. Is it new?

MISS TESMAN

I bought it for Hedda.

JORGEN

For Hedda?

MISS TESMAN

So that she won't be ashamed to be seen with me on the street.

JORGEN

(Pats her cheek) Aunt Ju, thoughtful as ever, what?

He puts the hat on a chair, sits MISS TESMAN down, and joins her.

MISS TESMAN

(Takes his hand) Oh, my dear, it's so good to have you back. Our precious one, home again, safe and sound.

JORGEN

And happy to be with my beloved Aunt Ju. Father and Mother to me for as long as I can remember. (Kisses her cheek.)

MISS TESMAN

So you won't forget your old Aunties?

JORGEN

How is Rina?

MISS TESMAN

Still the same. No change. All these years lying gazing up at the ceiling. Pray God she'll be spared for me to look after for a while yet. Now you've gone.

JORGEN

Now, now ... (Pats her hand.)

**MISS TESMAN**

(*Perking up*) I still can't believe it. Our little Jorgie. Married to Hedda Gabler. The Hedda Gabler! The most eligible girl in the district and she marries you!

**JORGEN**

Putting a few noses out of joint, what?

**MISS TESMAN**

And a six months' honeymoon. Six months!

**JORGEN**

But not all holidaying and sight-seeing Aunt. I was working, remember.

MISS TESMAN leans forward, confidential.

**MISS TESMAN**

Wonderful. Anything else?

**JORGEN**

Sorry?

**MISS TESMAN**

Any other news? No special little titbit for me?

**JORGEN**

About the honeymoon? I don't think so, no. You had it all in my letters. Except my special news. I wanted to keep that to tell you in person.

MISS TESMAN leans forward, smiling.

**JORGEN**

The doctorate! My doctorate, what?

**MISS TESMAN**

(*Sits back*) Oh yes, splendid! I just wondered if there was anything on the domestic front. Any hopes of ...

Come on, Jorgie, I'm your old Aunt, you can tell me. I
shan't say a word. Any expectations, as they say?

JORGEN

Actually, yes.

MISS TESMAN

I knew it!

JORGEN

Strictly between ourselves . . .

MISS TESMAN

Of course.

JORGEN

Aunt, I'm proud to say, you'll be happy to know that,
before long, I hope to be blessed with a Professorship.
But haven't I told you this?

MISS TESMAN

Of course you have, and very timely. A six-month
honeymoon must have been a dreadful drain on your
pocket.

JORGEN

I had my research grant.

MISS TESMAN

But that was for one. You had two people to support.
All the thing these days, honeymoons, I'm told. Well,
there you are. Now, have you had a chance to look
round the house?

JORGEN

I was up first thing.

MISS TESMAN

And the verdict?

JORGEN

A perfect property. The right setting for a striving academic. And decent enough for Hedda. Room for her to entertain ... and feel at home.

MISS TESMAN

I certainly hope so.

JORGEN

Tell me, what are the two little rooms leading off Hedda's bedroom?

MISS TESMAN

Darling boy. They're for something special ... very special ...

JORGEN

Oh, what? Oh! You mean my books.

MISS TESMAN

(Smiles) Yes, of course. Your books.

JORGEN

She had her heart set on this house. "It's the only house that I could possibly live in," she said. Never mind that it was already occupied and quite out of reach.

MISS TESMAN

Until the day after you left for your honeymoon and it came on the market!

JORGEN

Such incredible luck, what? Still hard to believe.

MISS TESMAN

Not that it won't be very expensive to run.

JORGEN

The rent's reasonable enough. Hedda says Judge
Brack's done well for us.

MISS TESMAN

He has. And I'm standing security for your furniture.
Rina and I are your guarantors.

JORGEN

*(Rises)* Juliane! Have you gone out of your mind?
That trust fund is all you and poor Rina have to live
on!

MISS TESMAN

Judge Brack assures me it's just a formality. Those
were his very words.

JORGEN

That may be so.

MISS TESMAN

In any case, you'll have a fine salary soon. Rina and I
don't mind going without in the meantime.

JORGEN

Oh Aunt. Will you ever stop making sacrifices for me?

MISS TESMAN

It's been a worthwhile cause. The prizes are in sight,
Jorgie.

JORGEN

Yes. Everything's working out beautifully, what?

MISS TESMAN

We've beaten the lot of them. Even him. *(He turns to
look at her.)* In the end, there was no need to worry.
He's ruined himself. You wouldn't wish it on any

of God's creatures but there it is. People end in the
gutter by their own choice.

JORGEN

(*After a pause*) How is Eilert? Any news of him?

MISS TESMAN

None at all. Well, except that he's published a book.

JORGEN

Eilert? Eilert Lvborg's written a book?

MISS TESMAN

So they say. It can't be up to much, can it? The way
things stand. Now, when you publish, there <u>will</u> be
something to celebrate. Have you finally settled on
your subject?

JORGEN

(*Abstracted*) Oh – yes.

MISS TESMAN

Good! At last! What's it to be?

JORGEN

I'm sorry? Oh, ah, I intend to cover the Brabantian
Domestic Industries, Rural and Urban, from 1446 to
1489. Inclusively.

MISS TESMAN

My word.

JORGEN

It'll be a while before I begin the book itself. There
is still a good deal of research to be done – not to
mention the organizing and indexing of material.

MISS TESMAN

Of course. Your dear father was just the same.
Everything had to be just so. Everything in the right
order.

JORGEN

I can't wait to get started now that I'm under my own
roof, with all the comforts of home.

MISS TESMAN

And your heart's desire. The girl you've always
dreamed of.

JORGEN

Yes. Hedda. The most wonderful, unbelievable success
of all. I still have to pinch myself. To think, Aunt Ju!
She chose me! Sssh, I think she's coming ...

HEDDA enters. She is tall, slender, grey-eyed and pale-skinned.
Her hair is chestnut, simply styled. She wears a morning gown.

HEDDA

Miss Tesman! So early. How kind.

MISS TESMAN

(Out of face) Not at all. Has the bride slept well in her
new bed?

HEDDA

Tolerably.

JORGEN

Tolerably? You were sleeping like a baby when I came
down.

HEDDA

If you say so. Oh!

JORGEN

What is it?

HEDDA

That fool of a maid has opened the windows.

MISS TESMAN

Allow me. (*She crosses to close the windows.*)

HEDDA

I'd rather you didn't. Leave the windows and draw the curtains, Tesman.

JORGEN crosses, draws the curtains across the open windows.

JORGEN

There. Shade and fresh air, what?

HEDDA

All these flowers! Do sit down, Miss Tesman.

MISS TESMAN

No, thank you. I just came to be sure you were settled. I must get back to my poor sister.

JORGEN

Give her my love. Tell her we'll be over later.

MISS TESMAN

Oh, I almost forgot. (*She gives JORGEN a package.*)

JORGEN

What's this? (*Opens the package*) Aunt Ju! You brought them! Hedda, look – my slippers! I missed them when we were away, remember? Aunt Rina embroidered them herself . . . do look.

HEDDA moves away.

MISS TESMAN

You can't expect them to mean the same to Hedda,
Jorgie.

JORGEN

Hedda's part of the family now.

HEDDA

Tesman, we really must dismiss that servant of
yours.

JORGEN

What? Berta? You mean Berta?

HEDDA

Look. Can you believe it? She's left her old hat on the
chair.

JORGEN

(Embarrassed, drops the slippers, whispers)
Hedda . . . !

HEDDA

Suppose someone came in and saw that thing sitting
there.

JORGEN

Hedda, that's Aunt Julla's hat.

HEDDA

Really.

MISS TESMAN picks up her hat.

MISS TESMAN

Yes, and it doesn't happen to be old. It happens to be
new, Miss Hedda.

HEDDA

I do beg your pardon. I should have looked more
closely.

MISS TESMAN

(*Putting it on*) It has never been worn until today.

JORGEN

And very handsome it is too. A magnificent hat,
what?

MISS TESMAN

Now you're being kind, dear boy. My new parasol. Ah,
here it is. This is mine as well. I don't think Berta has
laid claim to it.

JORGEN

A new hat and a new parasol, Hedda.

HEDDA

Very pretty.

JORGEN

Like someone else in this room, wouldn't you say,
Aunt Ju?

MISS TESMAN

Indeed. But that's not new. Hedda's been a beauty
from the day she was born. (*She makes to go.*)

JORGEN

(*Follows*) You don't notice a difference in her – a
special glow? She's filled out on honeymoon, wouldn't
you say?

HEDDA

(*Moving away*) Tesman, please.

JORGEN

You can't see it under that dress.

HEDDA

Because there's nothing to be seen.

JORGEN

It must be the mountain air, then.

HEDDA

Oh, leave it, Tesman. I'm exactly the same as when we left.

JORGEN

You're not, you know. Look, Aunt Ju, aren't I right?

MISS TESMAN inspects HEDDA.

MISS TESMAN

So beautiful.

She crosses, leans up, kisses HEDDA's cheek.

MISS TESMAN

God bless and keep you, for Jorgen's sake.

HEDDA evades her gently.

MISS TESMAN

I shall come and see you every day.

JORGEN

Absolutely.

MISS TESMAN

Goodbye ... goodbye ...

In the hall, we hear JORGEN thank his Aunt for the slippers and send his love to Aunt Rina.

HEDDA draws back the curtains and looks out at the garden.

JORGEN returns, and picks up his slippers.

JORGEN

What are you looking at?

HEDDA

The leaves are turning already.

JORGEN

September. I wonder what was the matter with Aunt
Ju?

HEDDA

No doubt it was the hat.

JORGEN

Surely not?

HEDDA

Throwing your clothes on a chair in someone else's
drawing room? Oh, I'll patch it up with her.

JORGEN

Would you?

HEDDA

Ask her back this evening when you visit.

JORGEN

Splendid! There is something else that would please
her enormously.

HEDDA

Oh?

JORGEN

Could you call her Aunt Julla like the rest of us? It
would make her so happy.

HEDDA

No.

JORGEN

For my sake.

HEDDA

No. Why must you insist? I may, possibly, bring myself to call her aunt in time. Further than that I cannot go.

JORGEN

But you're family now.

HEDDA

Am I? (*She moves away from him.*)

JORGEN

Is something wrong?

HEDDA

(*Points to the piano*) My piano. It doesn't look right in here.

JORGEN

As soon as my appointment comes through, I'll buy you a new one.

HEDDA

I'm fond of this old thing. We'll put it in the back room. The new one can go here.

JORGEN

Two pianos? If that's what you'd like.

HEDDA looks round the room and sees the flowers that Berta has just arranged.

HEDDA

These weren't here last night. *(She takes the card from the flowers, reads)* "I'll call you later today if I may." *(She turns over the card.)* Oh.

JORGEN

Who is it from?

HEDDA

It says 'Mrs Elvsted.'

JORGEN

Mrs Elvsted? Not the one who was Miss Rysing before she married?

HEDDA

Your old flame. Always tossing her hair about. Maddening woman.

JORGEN

*(Laughs)* My old flame! Only for a while and long before I met you. She's been living up north. Wonder what she's doing here?

HEDDA

And why she wants to see me. We haven't met since we were at school. *(Suddenly)* Doesn't <u>he</u> live up there?

JORGEN

I'm sorry?

HEDDA

Lvborg. Eilert Lvborg. He's been living in the north, hasn't he?

JORGEN

I believe so, yes.

BERTA enters.

> BERTA

The lady's here again, Madam. The one who come yesterday.

> HEDDA

Show her in.

BERTA goes and returns with MRS ELVSTED, bobs and exits.

MRS ELVSTED is a pretty woman, fine-featured, with a sensitive face and large blue eyes. She has glorious pale blonde hair. She is quietly dressed. HEDDA extends a hand.

> HEDDA

Mrs Elvsted, how nice to see you again!

> THEA ELVSTED

(Nervous) Yes – such a long time.

> JORGEN

(Holds out his hand) That goes for me too.

> HEDDA

Thank you for the lovely flowers.

> JORGEN

When did you arrive?

> THEA

Yesterday morning. I was so upset when they said you weren't here.

> HEDDA

Upset?

> JORGEN

My dear Miss Rysing – Mrs Elvsted I should say.

HEDDA

Is something the matter?

THEA

Yes, I'm afraid so. There's no-one else I can turn to.

HEDDA

Come and sit down.

THEA

Forgive me. I don't think I can. I'm too ...

HEDDA

Of course you can.

HEDDA pulls THEA down beside her. THEA puts down her large leather bag.

JORGEN

What is it Miss. Mrs ...?

HEDDA

Is there something wrong at home? Is this why you're here?

THEA

Yes. No.

HEDDA

Perhaps you had better tell us what's the matter.

JORGEN

Yes. What you've come about, Miss ... Mrs ...?

THEA

He's here.

JORGEN

Who?

HEDDA

Eilert Lvborg? (*To THEA*) You mean Eilert Lvborg?

THEA nods.

JORGEN

Good heavens. Eilert Lvborg's back. Did you hear that, Hedda?

HEDDA

How long has he been here?

THEA

A week.

HEDDA

You mean ... ?

THEA

Among people who are not good for him.

HEDDA

And you are worried?

THEA

Yes.

HEDDA

But is this any concern of yours? What has Eilert Lvborg to do with you?

MRS ELVSTED looks at her, frightened.

THEA

He ... he is a tutor to the children.

HEDDA

Children? Your children?

THEA

My husband's children. I have none of my own.

HEDDA

Your stepchildren?

THEA

Yes.

JORGEN

Tutor, did you say?

THEA

Yes.

JORGEN

Rather surprising. Is he – how shall I say – suitable
for such a post? In a fit state to be trusted with
children?

THEA

Oh yes. Mr Lvborg has been completely regular in his
habits for several years now.

JORGEN

Really? (*To HEDDA*) Did you hear that, Hedda?

HEDDA

I heard it, Tesman.

THEA

His behaviour has been irreproachable in every way.
It's simply that being here, in the city, with so much
money in his pockets, I'm worried that something
may happen.

JORGEN

Why is he here?

THEA

The book.

JORGEN

Aunt Julla told us that he'd published.

THEA

You didn't know? Of course, you've been abroad.

JORGEN

What is it about?

THEA

Mr Tesman, you must read it. It's a huge success. The shops are selling out – and rightly so. It's a history of civilisation.

JORGEN

Something he dug up from better days I presume. Before he, well, became less competent, what?

THEA

Oh no, not at all. It's a new work. He wrote it under our roof all last year. It's entirely new material.

JORGEN

Really? Well, splendid. Good news eh, Hedda?

THEA

And everything has gone well. Very well. It's simply that, not being with us – being here – you do see what I mean?

HEDDA

Where is he?

THEA

I don't know. I can't find him.

HEDDA

And your husband? What does he think of all this?

THEA

My husband?

HEDDA

Does he mind your leaving the children, travelling all this way? I'm surprised he didn't come himself, given the circumstances.

THEA

Oh no. He's ... he's very busy. And I wanted to do some shopping.

HEDDA

(*Smiles*) Oh well, that's different.

THEA

(*Rises, restless*) Mr Tesman, if he should come to see you, which I'm sure he will since you're such good friends ...

JORGEN

Well, we were.

THEA

You must still have so much in common, working in the same field. Could I ask you to keep a friendly eye on him? As a colleague.

JORGEN

Gladly, Miss Rysing.

HEDDA

Mrs Elvsted.

JORGEN

Anything I can do to help Eilert shall be done. Count on me.

THEA

Thank you so much. I knew I only had to ask.
(*Nervous*) It's just that – my husband is so fond of
Eilert.

HEDDA

(*Rises*) Send a note, Tesman. He may not call
otherwise.

JORGEN

That's it!

HEDDA

Why not now?

JORGEN

Splendid. Do you have an address, Mrs Elvsted?

THEA

(*Takes out a paper*) I'm told he's staying there.

JORGEN

Thank you.

HEDDA

Do write a long, friendly letter rather than a note. He
may need encouragement.

JORGEN

Very good, ma'am.

THEA

Oh, and Mr Tesman, if you wouldn't mind not
mentioning my name? I'd rather he didn't know I'd
spoken to you.

JORGEN

I shan't say a word.

He goes into the back room. HEDDA closes on THEA.

            HEDDA
There. Two birds with one stone.

            THEA
How do you mean?

            HEDDA
We've got rid of Tesman. Now we can talk properly.
(*She waits*) Well?

            THEA
I'm sorry? You mean about Mr Lvborg? There's really
nothing more to tell.

            HEDDA
Oh, I think there is. I think there's a great deal more.
Come and sit down.

She takes THEA by the arm, sits her down, and draws up a footstool
at her side.

            THEA
(*Looking at her watch*) I really ought to be going, Mrs
Tesman.

            HEDDA
There's no hurry. We must catch up. How are things
with you at home?

            THEA
At home? I'd really rather not say.

            HEDDA
My dear, you can tell me. We were at school together!

            THEA
But you were ahead of me. In fact, I was afraid of you.

HEDDA

Of me? Why?

THEA

I found you rather frightening.

HEDDA

Frightening?

THEA

Whenever we met on the stairs, you would pull my
hair.

HEDDA

Surely not.

THEA

Don't you remember? You pinned me against the wall
once and said you were going to burn it all off.

HEDDA

That was just a tease!

THEA

Perhaps, but I was silly enough to believe you.
Anyway, those days are over. Since then our lives
have taken us in different directions.

HEDDA

Then it's time to close the gap. Renew old
acquaintance. We must get back to using Christian
names again.

THEA

Oh, I don't think we ever did that.

HEDDA

Of course we did. You and I must be friends. Tell all
our secrets. Why not? We all need friends. *(She leans,*

and *kisses THEA on the cheek*) You must call me
Hedda.

**THEA**
(*Grasps HEDDA's hand*) Thank you. I have so few
friends.

**HEDDA**
And I shall call you Thora.

**THEA**
Thea. My name is Thea.

**HEDDA**
Of course. Thea. I meant Thea. You've no friends,
Thea? Not even at home?

**THEA**
Home? Is there such a word? I have no home.

**HEDDA**
You see, I was right. I knew it.

**THEA**
I have never had a home.

**HEDDA**
You went north as your husband's housekeeper, did
you not?

**THEA**
As governess, supposedly. But his wife was an
invalid, so I had to take on everything else.

**HEDDA**
And in the end, you became mistress of the house?

THEA

(*Heavily*) Yes. I married Elvsted after the first Mrs
Elvsted died.

HEDDA

When was that?

THEA

Five years ago. Five long years. The last two
unbearable. Oh, Mrs Tesman, if you only knew!

HEDDA

Hedda, Thea, Hedda!

THEA

I'm sorry, I'll try.

HEDDA

(*Casually*) How long has Eilert been with you? Two,
three years?

THEA

About that.

HEDDA

Did you know him before?

THEA

Only by name.

HEDDA

Does he live in the house?

THEA

No. He comes every day to teach the children.

HEDDA

What about your husband? As a country magistrate, I
imagine he is away a lot.

THEA

Yes, he has the whole district to cover.

HEDDA

(*Leans forward*) My poor Thea. Now you must tell me everything. All of it. Just between ourselves.

THEA

What do you want to know?

HEDDA

Your husband. What is he like? Does he look after you?

THEA

(*Evasive*) He does his best.

HEDDA

He's twenty years older than you, I believe.

THEA

That doesn't help ... oh, there are so many things! We're completely different in every way. We've nothing in common at all.

HEDDA

But, surely he cares for you?

THEA

I'm useful to him. I cost very little, I'm a good bargain.

HEDDA

Surely you don't mean ...?

THEA

He cares for no-one but himself. Perhaps the children a little.

HEDDA

But he must be fond of Eilert.

THEA

Mr Lvborg? What makes you say that?

HEDDA

To send you all the way here to look for him. Wasn't that what you told Tesman? That your husband had sent you?

THEA

Did I? Yes, I suppose I must. *(Low and rapid)* You may as well know the truth, Mrs Tesman. It's bound to come out.

HEDDA waits.

THEA

My husband has no idea that I am here.

HEDDA

He doesn't know?

THEA

He was away on circuit when I left.

HEDDA

You left home?

THEA

As soon as his carriage had turned the corner.

HEDDA

Did you tell anyone?

THEA shakes her head.

HEDDA

That was very brave. What will he do, your husband,
when he finds you've gone?

THEA

I'm never going back.

HEDDA

You've left everything? Your home? Everything? For
good?

THEA

I had to.

HEDDA

Don't you mind what people will say?

THEA

(Sits) Whatever they say, I shan't go back.

HEDDA

How will you survive?

THEA

I don't know. All I know is that as long as I'm near him
I am alive.

HEDDA

Him?

THEA

He is all that matters.

HEDDA

Eilert Lvborg. (She rises, paces.) Yes. When did all
this start? How did it begin?

THEA

Between Eilert and me? Slowly at first, and then,
somehow, I began to . . . to influence him.

HEDDA

You? How?

THEA

I persuaded him not to drink.

HEDDA

How in the name of Hades did you manage that?

THEA

I don't know.

HEDDA

You must have done something.

THEA

We never . . . I never confronted him. He simply . . .

HEDDA

What?

THEA

I think he saw that it upset me.

HEDDA

So he stopped? He stopped drinking?

THEA

Yes.

HEDDA

For you? For little Thea? He became a new man
because of you?

THEA

That is what he says. But he changed me. I am not at
all what I was. I understand so much because of him.

HEDDA

He's been your tutor as well as the children's?

THEA

Yes. Helping him in his work has changed my life.

HEDDA

You help him? With his writing?

THEA

We work together as colleagues . . . and friends.

HEDDA

Friends?

THEA

He believes in friendship. In a true, open, close
relationship between a man and a woman.

HEDDA

So you are . . . friends. All's well between you. He is
here and you have left your husband to be near him.
So? What is the matter? Why aren't you happy?

THEA shakes her head.

HEDDA

Why not?

THEA

I am afraid.

HEDDA

You don't trust him?

THEA

As much as he trusts himself.

HEDDA

Yes. I see. You're not certain.

THEA

There's something else. A woman.

HEDDA

Woman?

THEA

Standing between us. A woman he once knew.

HEDDA

(*Leans forward*) Who?

THEA

I don't know, but she's still in his mind.

HEDDA

Does he say that? Has he said that?

THEA

Once. I asked him about her.

HEDDA

What did he say?

THEA

Nothing, except that she had red hair.

HEDDA

Red hair. Did he say who she was?

THEA

No. Only that he left her, and she tried to shoot him
with a pistol.

HEDDA

Nonsense.

THEA

No, it's possible. There was a singer with red hair. I
remember her. She lived here. People said she carried
a gun. I've been told she's living here again.

HEDDA

Ssh! Tesman's coming. Not a word, Thea.

THEA

Heavens, no.

JORGEN enters, his letter in his hand.

JORGEN

My letter, all signed and sealed.

HEDDA

Mrs Elvsted is leaving. (*to THEA*) I'll walk you to the
gate.

BERTA enters.

BERTA

Judge Brack's outside, Madam.

HEDDA

Then ask him to come in. (*She takes the letter from
JORGEN*) And put this in the letter box.

BERTA

(*Takes the letter*) Very good, Madam. (*She ushers in
JUDGE BRACK and goes.*)

BRACK enters. He is in his forties, strongly-built, well-dressed – a
composed, alive man.

JUDGE BRACK

May one make an appearance so early in the day?

HEDDA

One may.

JORGEN

Judge, you're always welcome! (*He shakes BRACK's hand.*) Judge Brack. Miss Rysing.

HEDDA groans

JORGEN

I beg your pardon, Mrs Elvsted.

BRACK

(*Bows*) Delighted.

HEDDA

We don't often see you in the morning.

BRACK

Not too startling, I hope.

HEDDA

People look so different in daylight.

BRACK

Oh dear. In what way?

HEDDA

(*Surveys him*) Younger.

BRACK

I must remember.

JORGEN

What do you think of Hedda, Judge? Blooming, what?

HEDDA

Oh, be quiet. And do thank the Judge for all the
trouble he's been to.

BRACK

Pure pleasure, I assure you.

HEDDA

A true friend. But my other friend is dying to be on
her way.

HEDDA offers her hand to BRACK, and then exits with THEA.

BRACK

(*Bows as they leave*) So, is the bride pleased with her
new house?

JORGEN

Oh yes, we can't thank you enough for all the work
you've put in. Shall we sit down?

BRACK

Thank you. There is something I'd like to discuss.

JORGEN

Of course. After the celebrations, the adding up,
what?

BRACK

Oh, no hurry. Though it might have been wiser to hold
back for the time being.

JORGEN

My dear chap, we can't expect Hedda to settle for
anything but the best.

BRACK

That does pose a problem.

JORGEN

Which will be solved as soon as my appointment is
confirmed.

BRACK

These things can take time, Tesman.

JORGEN

Any more news?

BRACK

Yes. Your old friend Eilert Lvborg is back.

JORGEN

So I've heard.

BRACK

Oh? How?

JORGEN

The lady who was here with Hedda told us.

BRACK

Indeed? I didn›t catch her name.

JORGEN

Mrs Elvsted. Miss Rysing that was.

BRACK

Elvsted? Ah, the magistrate's wife. I hear Lvborg's
been living with them.

JORGEN

As a reformed character, I gather. And he's published
a book!

BRACK

Oh yes. It's created quite a stir.

JORGEN

Splendid, what? Eilert was always a gifted chap. It's good to hear that his talents aren't going to waste. I rather thought he was finished.

BRACK

So did we all.

JORGEN

Is he managing to survive?

HEDDA enters, and laughs.

HEDDA

Tesman always wonders how people make ends meet.

JORGEN

My dear! We were talking about poor old Lvborg. He can hardly survive on the income from one book. And he's run through all the family money . . .

BRACK

His relatives aren't without influence.

JORGEN

Oh, they gave him up long ago.

BRACK

Blood is blood. He is still regarded as the hope of the family.

JORGEN

Seriously?

HEDDA

(Laughs) And who knows? Perhaps country life and the Elvsteds have worked a miracle.

BRACK

There is the new book. If he's working again ...

JORGEN

Perhaps we can find something for him. By the way,
I've asked him round for this evening, Hedda.

BRACK

Tonight, my dear chap, you're dining with me. Don't
you remember?

HEDDA

Your welcome party. Had you forgotten?

JORGEN

Good heavens. So I had!

BRACK

Lvborg's hardly likely to appear, in any case.

HEDDA

Oh? Why not?

BRACK

There is something that ... (*Hesitates*) Well, I've
heard that ... Put it this way. Your appointment as
professor may not be as certain as you've been led to
expect.

JORGEN

(*Rises*) Why, what's happened? Is something wrong?

BRACK

There may be a competition for the post.

JORGEN

Competition? Why? How? Did you hear that, Hedda?

HEDDA

(*Sits back*) Yes. I see.

JORGEN

A competition? With whom? You're not saying...?

BRACK

Afraid so. Eilert Lvborg.

JORGEN

No. That's unthinkable!

BRACK

Nonetheless...

JORGEN

No, no. Out of the question, Judge. I'd be in an
impossible position. Good Lord, man, I got married
on the strength of this appointment. We've taken on
debt, borrowed from the Aunts. The chair was as good
as promised! As you know.

BRACK

Oh, you'll get it, no question. It's just a formality. A
matter of making yourself available to opposition.

HEDDA

A fight? That'll be fun.

BRACK

In the meantime, it might be wise to defer any
expenditure on the improvements to the house, Mrs
Tesman.

HEDDA

Why?

BRACK

Your decision, of course. Forgive me, I must get on. I'll
call for you later, Tesman. Till then, eh?

JORGEN

Yes, yes. I'm sorry. I can't think straight.

HEDDA

(*Holds out her hand*) You are always welcome.

BRACK

Too kind. Goodbye for now.

JORGEN

(*Seeing him out*) Goodbye . . . goodbye.

BRACK goes.

JORGEN

There we are, Hedda. So much for dreams of glory.

HEDDA

(*Smiling*) Oh dear. Is that what they've been?

JORGEN

Getting married, setting up house on the promise of
expectations. At all events, we have this place. I've
got you the house you wanted. I've been so looking
forward to seeing you in your element. Dinners,
musical evenings. Now, for the time being, it seems
we must settle for each other's company. And Aunt
Julla's of course. I know this is not what you had in
mind.

HEDDA

Are you saying there's to be no manservant?

JORGEN

Heavens no. We couldn't possibly take on a footman
with this over our heads.

HEDDA

What about the mare? My horse. It was part of the
arrangement. Do you mean I can't have the mare?

JORGEN

Not until our situation is clarified, I'm afraid.

HEDDA walks away. She turns.

HEDDA

In that case, there's only one amusement left.

JORGEN

Amusement?

She turns to the back room.

HEDDA

(Calls) My father's pistols.

JORGEN

(Calls) Hedda please! For heavens' sake, don't touch
those. They're dangerous! Hedda, are you there?
Hedda, please!

*Fade to black.*

ACT TWO

The same setting as before. The piano is gone. In its place stands an elegant writing table with drawers. HEDDA, dressed for callers, is by the open window. She is loading a pistol.

HEDDA

(*Calls*) Good evening!

BRACK

(*Offstage*) Hullo again!

HEDDA

Stand still.

BRACK

Why?

HEDDA

I'm going to shoot you.

She fires.

BRACK

(*Calls*) Have you gone completely mad?

HEDDA

It serves you right for sneaking in the back way.

BRACK enters. He is dressed for dinner, and carries a light overcoat.

HEDDA

Did I hit you?

BRACK

What the hell were you aiming at?

316

HEDDA

The sky.

BRACK

You're not still fooling around with those things? (*He holds out his hand.*)

She gives him the pistol.

BRACK

Ah. I recognise this. (*He sees the case, and puts the pistol away.*) I think we've had enough games for today.

HEDDA

What do you suggest I do with myself?

BRACK

Tesman not in?

HEDDA

Gone to see his beloved Aunts.

BRACK

Ah, yes. If I'd known he was going to be out I'd have come earlier.

HEDDA

You would have found an empty room. I was dressing.

BRACK

I see. No little crack in the door we might have talked through?

HEDDA

You didn't have one built in.

BRACK

Another stupidity.

HEDDA

Tesman won't be back for some time, I'm afraid.

BRACK

What a bore. I must contain myself with patient
resignation.

HEDDA sits on the corner of the sofa. BRACK puts his coat over a
chair and sits. They look at each other.

HEDDA

Well?

BRACK

*(Same tone)* Well?

HEDDA

I asked first.

BRACK

Very pleasant. A little time together, Mrs Tesman.
I've been looking forward to your reappearance.

HEDDA

No more than I have.

BRACK

Were you not enjoying yourself? According to
Tesman's letters . . .

HEDDA

According to Tesman, every day was more blissful
than the last. Months of enchantment, buried in
parchments from every library in Europe.

BRACK

It is his raison d'être.

HEDDA

His. Not mine.

BRACK

You were less enchanted.

HEDDA

Water torture.

BRACK

Really? That bad?

HEDDA

One asks oneself: who on earth conceived the notion of matrimony! The idea of being attached for the rest of one's life. Being presented, week after week, month after month, year after ... with the <u>same face</u>.

BRACK

But, surely, he's a distinguished man, Tesman. Is he not?

HEDDA

He's an academic.

BRACK

Point taken.

HEDDA

A scavenger. And a scavenger obsessed with one pointless subject. One subject! The rest of the world invisible. Not the most amusing company.

BRACK

Even when one is in love?

HEDDA

Don't be ludicrous. 'The Domestic Industries and Crafts of Brabant, 1446 to 1489.' – Ach!

BRACK

(*Pause*) If that's the way it is … if you feel like that …

HEDDA

Why did I marry?

BRACK

Yes.

HEDDA

You find it surprising?

BRACK

Inexplicable.

HEDDA

(*After a pause.*) I was running out of time. No, I mustn't say that. I mustn't even think it. After all, what's wrong with Tesman? His background is respectable, wouldn't you say?

BRACK

No question of it.

HEDDA

And he's not ridiculous, is he?

BRACK

Ridiculous? No, I wouldn't say ridiculous.

HEDDA

He's said to be skilled at all this – whatever he does. Who knows? He could even end up with some status.

BRACK

That's the general opinion. Which presumably you share.

HEDDA

(*Tired*) I must do. When he begged to provide for me, there seemed no reason not to say yes. It was more than any of my other admirers were prepared to offer.

BRACK

I've the greatest respect for the institution of marriage. For other people.

HEDDA

Oh, I never had any hopes of you.

BRACK

All I ask is a circle of friends. People I can be of use to, in one way or another. To be able to come and go. Be welcome where I feel comfortable, in the houses of those I admire.

HEDDA

Welcomed by the husbands and the wives?

BRACK

Perhaps more by the wives. But the husbands, too, of course. My ideal – how can I describe it? – is a three-way friendship. Yes. That sort of arrangement can be very satisfying for all concerned.

HEDDA

What I wouldn't have given for another companion on those endless journeys! Mile after mile in railway carriages, looking at each other.

BRACK

Well. Over now.

HEDDA

Over? How can you say so? I'm still on the train.
Stuck in a compartment in a siding inside a tunnel,
inside a mountain.

BRACK

Then jump out, Mrs Hedda. Take the air.

HEDDA

Not my style.

BRACK

Are you concerned for your reputation?

HEDDA

Let's just say that I prefer to stay inside the
compartment.

BRACK

(*After a pause.*) What if you had company?

HEDDA

Company?

BRACK

Someone to step in and join you. An old, trusted
friend.

HEDDA

Who was amusing and full of life?

BRACK

And who promised not one reference to the Burghers
of Brabant.

HEDDA

That would be ... pleasant.

BRACK

(*Hears the door*) The circle is complete. The train has
taken on water and can move on.

JORGEN enters, arms and pockets full of soft-backed books. He
spills them out onto the table.

JORGEN

It's too hot for this. Look at me, I'm sweating, Hedda.
Ah, you're here already, Judge. Berta didn't say.

BRACK

(*Rising*) I came through the garden.

HEDDA

What on earth are all those?

JORGEN

(*Glancing through them*) New journals. I had to get
them. They deal with my subject.

BRACK

Brabant? In the Middle Ages?

JORGEN

Background material.

HEDDA

Haven't you enough already?

JORGEN

Oh, you can never have enough. It's important to
keep up, Hedda. Essential. Look. I bought Eilert's
book. Would you like to see it? I had a peep on my way
home.

BRACK

And what's the verdict?

JORGEN

Oh, very sound! A remarkable piece of work. A great step on from his earlier stuff, very wide-ranging. (*Gathers the books*) I'll just take these through. Such a joy cutting the pages. Oh, I shall need to change. We're in no hurry, are we, Judge?

BRACK

No. Take your time.

JORGEN

(*Makes to go*) Splendid. (*Stops*) Oh, Hedda. Aunt Ju won't be coming tonight.

HEDDA

Still upset about the hat?

JORGEN

Aunt Ju? How could you think such a thing? No, I'm afraid it's Aunt Rina.

BRACK

Not well?

HEDDA

She never is.

JORGEN

But today not well at all, I'm afraid.

HEDDA

Then of course the other one must be with her.

JORGEN

Aunt Ju sends her love. She was so taken with how well you looked!

HEDDA

(*Rises, mutters*) Oh God save me from Aunts!

JORGEN

I beg your pardon?

HEDDA

(*At the window*) Nothing.

JORGEN

Right.

JORGEN goes.

BRACK

What was that about the hat?

HEDDA

(*Laughs*) The aunt's hat. She left it on the chair this morning. I pretended I thought it was the maid's.

BRACK

Mrs Tesman, how could you?

HEDDA

(*On the move*) Impossible to stop oneself. Oh, never explain.

She sits. BRACK stands behind the chair.

BRACK

The explanation is simple. You are unhappy.

HEDDA

(*Pause*) How could I not be?

BRACK

(*Shrugs*) You've got this place. The house you've always wanted.

HEDDA

You really believe that?

BRACK

Is it not true?

HEDDA

(*Pause*) Last year, when Tesman began to bring me home from parties ...

BRACK

Such a pity I lived in the opposite direction ...

HEDDA

Oh, your interests were entirely elsewhere that summer.

They laugh.

HEDDA

We were passing this house one night and Tesman was trying to make conversation, so I said – for something to say – that I'd always wanted to live here. I might as easily have said that I liked frogs.

BRACK

I see.

HEDDA

One frivolous sentence, clawed out of an empty silence, and look at the consequences.

BRACK

Frivolous things can do that. Turn into something else altogether.

HEDDA

Anyway, it was the house that drew us together. Out of nowhere, there was suddenly an understanding, which led inexorably to an engagement and 'Mr and Mrs Jorgen Tesman are touring on an extended

honeymoon. Poste Restante.' I have, as they say,
made my bed.

                    BRACK

Didn't you want the house at all?

                    HEDDA

God no!

                    BRACK

So, we've all been to a lot of trouble for nothing! You
don't like the place?

                    HEDDA

It smells of death. I am so bored.

                    BRACK

Find something to do.

                    HEDDA

What?

                    BRACK

Anything that interests you.

                    HEDDA

(*After a pause.*) I did think of sending Tesman into
politics.

                    BRACK

Politics? Jorgen? He'd never survive.

                    HEDDA

You're right, of course.

                    BRACK

For a start, he hasn't enough money. You need to be a
rich man.

### HEDDA

(*Rises*) Oh, this wretched shortage of money!

### BRACK

That's not the problem.

### HEDDA

Yes, it is. If we had money ...

### BRACK

(*Shrugs*) To be wealthier is simply to have larger debts. You would spend and be just as miserable. Look at you, Mrs Hedda. What has ever happened to you? What have you done? What has inspired you, engaged you, taken your breath away? You sit in your bell-tower, waiting for life to unfold like the thrilling cavalcade that you believe, as a woman, to be your birthright. But what risks have you taken? What hazards have you faced? Well, perhaps some of those are about to happen.

### HEDDA

You mean poor Tesman's appointment? The competition? That's his business. It doesn't concern me.

### BRACK

Does it not? Very well, what about a new sort of demand? A new ... personal ... responsibility?

### HEDDA

Shut up.

### BRACK

We'll talk about it later, Mrs Married Lady. In a year's time, perhaps?

HEDDA

I have absolutely no intentions in that direction.

BRACK

Surely, it's a woman's destiny?

HEDDA

My talents lie elsewhere.

BRACK

And where would that be?

HEDDA

In boring myself to death. (*Laughs*) Here he comes,
the Professor ...

BRACK

Now, now, Mrs Hedda ...

JORGEN enters in evening clothes.

JORGEN

Good evening, good evening! Any message from
Eilert?

HEDDA

None.

JORGEN

If he hasn't sent a refusal, he'll be here for sure.

BRACK

You think so?

JORGEN

Oh yes. And what you were saying this morning –
there's nothing in it, you know. Eilert wouldn't stand
in my way. Aunt Julla says so.

BRACK

Then all is well.

JORGEN

Do you mind if we hang on? I'd like to say hullo to
him.

BRACK

Not at all.

JORGEN

Eilert could join us at dinner, what?

HEDDA

He may prefer to keep me company.

JORGEN

Oh, I don't think so. Aunt Ju won't be here, remember.
It would be just the two of you.

HEDDA

Not at all. I'm expecting Mrs Elvsted.

JORGEN

Ah – fine.

BERTA

(*At the door*) There's another gentleman out there,
Madam.

HEDDA

Well, show him in!

BERTA

Show him in? (*Going*) ... show him in ...

EILERT LVBORG enters. He is lean and gaunt in dark clothes.

He stops by the door, and bows abruptly. JORGEN crosses,
extending his arms.

JORGEN

My dear Eilert. It's good to see you after all this time!

LVBORG

(*Quietly*) Thank you for your note. Hedda. (*He corrects himself*) Mrs Tesman.

HEDDA offers her hand, inclining her head.

HEDDA

Judge, do you and Mr Lvborg ...?

BRACK

(*Bows slightly*) I believe our paths have crossed.

LVBORG

Judge Brack.

JORGEN

I hear you're back with us again?

LVBORG

Yes.

JORGEN

You must treat this house as your own, mustn't he, Hedda? Look, I've just got it – your book. I can't wait to start reading it.

LVBORG

Oh, don't bother with that.

JORGEN

Why not?

LVBORG

It doesn't say anything.

JORGEN

What?!

BRACK

I'm told it's had a very good reception.

LVBORG

That was the intention. To publish something acceptable.

BRACK

A good idea.

JORGEN

Indeed. Re-establish yourself, what?

LVBORG

(Takes a package from his pocket) Read this.

JORGEN

What is it?

LVBORG

The sequel.

JORGEN

Sequel?

LVBORG

To the other book.

JORGEN

But doesn't that cover the subject to the present day?

LVBORG

This is about the future.

JORGEN

The future? I don't understand. How can we write anything about the future? It hasn't happened. We don't know anything about the future.

LVBORG

Don't we? (*Takes out the manuscript from its wrapper.*) Take a look.

JORGEN

(*Takes the manuscript*) This isn't your handwriting.

LVBORG

I dictated it. (*Turns the pages*) There are two sections. A survey of modernism in the physical, commercial and industrial sense. And how civilisation is likely to be affected.

JORGEN

Amazing.

LVBORG

I was hoping to read some of it this evening.

JORGEN

Splendid! Oh, alas, this evening ...

BRACK

I'm giving a party for Tesman tonight.

LVBORG

Some other time then.

BRACK

Please, do join us.

LVBORG

(*Abrupt*) Thank you, no.

BRACK

Bring the manuscript with you. You can read it to Tesman in another room.

JORGEN

That's an idea.

HEDDA

Perhaps Mr Lvborg would prefer to stay and have
supper with me?

LVBORG

With you?

HEDDA

And Mrs Elvsted.

LVBORG

Mrs Elvsted?

HEDDA

Now you must stay, Mr Lvborg, or she'll have no-one
to escort her home.

LVBORG

In that case.

HEDDA crosses and rings. BERTA enters. HEDDA speaks to her.
She nods and goes through to the back room. During this, the
three men talk.

JORGEN

So, Eilert. This subject of yours. I hear you've planned
a series of lectures this autumn?

LVBORG

You don't mind?

JORGEN

Good heavens. Of course not.

LVBORG

I don't want to muddy the ground for you. If you
prefer, I'll wait until you've been appointed.

JORGEN

Wait? Surely that's not in your interest? Not if you're
standing for the post yourself.

LVBORG

Oh, I've no ambitions there.

BRACK

Have you not?

LVBORG

None at all.

BRACK

A man without ambition?

LVBORG

I didn't say that.

BRACK

Then where would you say they lie, your ambitions?

LVBORG

In people's hearts ... minds.

JORGEN calls to HEDDA in the back room, who is talking to BERTA.

JORGEN

Do you hear that Hedda? It's splendid. Eilert has no
intention of standing in my way. What about that?

HEDDA

Bravo. A glass of punch, gentlemen. (She indicates the
back room.) Mr Lvborg?

LVBORG

Thank you, no.

BRACK

One glass of punch won't do you any harm.

HEDDA

Perhaps Mr Lvborg prefers my company?

She waves JORGEN and BRACK into the back room.

LVBORG pauses, then sits.

HEDDA

Now. How to amuse ourselves? Let me see. I know.
Photographs! Would you like to see some photographs
of our extended foreign outing? Of course! Who
wouldn't?

She fetches a LARGE PHOTOGRAPH ALBUM, and sits beside him.

HEDDA

Let me see. (*Turns pages*) Ah. The Orton Mountains.
There – Tesman has written the name underneath.
'The Orton Mountains, near Meran.'

LVBORG

(*Looks at her steadily*) Hedda – Gabler.

HEDDA

Sssh.

LVBORG

Hedda Gabler.

HEDDA

That was my name when we knew each other. Not
anymore.

LVBORG

Hedda Gabler. I must teach myself not to say it.

HEDDA

(*Turning a page*) The sooner the better.

LVBORG

Hedda Gabler. Married to Jorgen Tesman.

HEDDA

Yes. Jorgen Tesman!

LVBORG

When? How? Why? How could you do it? Throw
yourself away – sell yourself?

HEDDA

(*Whispers*) Stop it.

JORGEN enters.

HEDDA

This is the Ampezzo Valley, do look at the peaks.
What were they called, my dear?

JORGEN

Let me have a look. Oh yes, those are the Dolomites.

HEDDA

That's it – the Dolomites, Mr Lvborg.

JORGEN

A glass of punch, Hedda?

HEDDA

Please.

JORGEN

Cigarette?

HEDDA

No.

JORGEN

Very good.

He rejoins BRACK in the back room, who has been watching them.

LVBORG

(Softly) Hedda . . .

HEDDA

(Turning the pages) You can't call me that any more.

LVBORG

Not even when we're alone?

HEDDA

You can think it, but you can't say it.

LVBORG

Because you love Jorgen Tesman.

HEDDA

Love Tesman? Are you trying to be funny?

LVBORG

You don't love Jorgen Tesman?

HEDDA

Nor do I intend to betray him.

JORGEN appears with a tray.

JORGEN

Refreshments!

HEDDA

Why didn't you ask Berta?

JORGEN

(*Filling glasses*) I like waiting on you myself.

HEDDA

(*As he pours a second glass*) Not for Mr Lvborg.

JORGEN

This is for Mrs Elvsted, had you forgotten?

HEDDA

We were looking at pictures. Remember the little village?

JORGEN

Under the Brenner Pass. We spend the night there.

HEDDA

And met some amusing people for once.

JORGEN

I'm sorry you weren't with us, Eilert. We had a splendid time.

JORGEN leaves the drinks tray, and returns to the back room to rejoin BRACK.

LVBORG

One thing I need to know.

HEDDA

And what is that?

LVBORG

Were you not in love with me either? Hedda?

HEDDA

What we had – our friendship – your opening your heart to me. No man had ever done that before. Told everything.

LVBORG

At the time, the insistence, I seem to remember, was
yours.

HEDDA

Remember how we sat on the sofa, the General across
the room reading his paper, while we turned the
pages of a magazine – always the same one.

LVBORG

You had everything from me. The drinking ... the
women. Why? What made me do that?

HEDDA

Perhaps I cast a spell over you?

LVBORG

Always questions. Nothing direct, just foraging,
oblique – everything implied.

HEDDA

Oblique? Implied? You knew perfectly well what I
wanted. And what you couldn't wait to tell me.

LVBORG

You walked straight in. What I don't understand,
looking back, were your motives. You must have
cared. Why else would you want to know everything,
if not to haul me out of the crevasse, give me the
strength to change my life. You must have cared.
Didn't you?

HEDDA

Not really.

LVBORG

Then why?

HEDDA

I was young. I wasn't supposed to know anything.
About anything.

LVBORG

And that was it. You were curious. (*Pause.*)
So, you didn't love me. You wanted
information – experience – second-hand.

HEDDA

Obviously, I hoped to make a difference, have some
influence over you.

LVBORG

In that case, why did you break it off?

HEDDA

That was you.

LVBORG

No. You put an end to it. Why?

HEDDA

It was getting out of control.

LVBORG

We were falling in love!

HEDDA

I couldn't have that. Being infected by you. Taken
over. It had to stop.

LVBORG

Why didn't you shoot me? You threatened to.

HEDDA

Oh, I would have.

LVBORG

But you didn't. That you spared me must have meant
something.

HEDDA

Not at all. I preferred not to risk a scandal.

LVBORG

You're a coward.

HEDDA

Perhaps. However, I believe you've found more than
adequate consolation. Mrs Elvsted?

LVBORG

Who says so?

HEDDA

She does.

LVBORG

I see. You've been talking to her.

HEDDA

As no doubt you have.

LVBORG

From time to time.

HEDDA

Telling her about me?

LVBORG

God no.

HEDDA

Why not, if she's your confidante? Haven't you told
her everything?

LVBORG

No.

HEDDA

Why ever not?

LVBORG

She wouldn't understand. She's naive.

HEDDA

I see. Naive. She's a fool and I'm a coward. (*She looks into his eyes.*) Would you like to know why I didn't kill you?

They gaze at each other intensely.

HEDDA

(*Softly*) It wasn't the only cowardly thing I did. Or didn't do. That night.

He turns, taking her meaning, and moves in on her.

LVBORG

Oh Hedda! Can't you see? Don't you understand? What you were looking for was Life! Life.

He tries to embrace her. She removes herself.

HEDDA

That's enough. We'll have no more of that.

LVBORG

Please ...

HEDDA

No! Don't delude yourself ... don't!

BERTA ushers in THEA.

HEDDA

Thea! How lovely. At last. I thought you were never coming.

THEA bows to BRACK and TESMAN within, who rise and bow.

LVBORG rises. He and THEA nod to each other briefly.

HEDDA

(Indicates for THEA to sit) My husband and the Judge are just leaving. Off to enjoy themselves. A 'welcome home' party.

THEA

(Alarmed, to LVBORG) Will you be joining them?

HEDDA

Mr Lvborg will be staying. He prefers our company.

THEA, relieved, makes to sit by LVBORG.

HEDDA

No, no. Come and sit here, Thea dear. Then I can be between you. Enjoy you both.

They sit. A pause. LVBORG looks at THEA then at HEDDA.

LVBORG

Rather lovely, don't you think?

HEDDA strokes THEA'S hair.

HEDDA

And not only to look at, it seems.

LVBORG

Mrs Elvsted and I are good friends.

HEDDA

Totally open? No foraging? Nothing oblique?

THEA

Oh, Hedda, he's made me so happy. He says I've been
his inspiration. He truly believes that.

HEDDA

Does he?

LVBORG

She has courage, Mrs Tesman.

HEDDA

Thea, a glass of cold punch.

THEA

Thank you no, I never touch it.

HEDDA

You will, Mr Lvborg?

LVBORG

Thank you, no.

HEDDA

And if I want you to?

LVBORG

The answer would still be no.

THEA

He doesn't drink.

HEDDA

Oh! Have I no power over you?

LVBORG

Not where this is concerned.

HEDDA

Surely one glass. For my sake. And your own.

THEA

Hedda!

HEDDA

Refusing the Judge's invitation to dinner, people may
think you don't trust yourself.

LVBORG

People can think what they like.

THEA

(*Low*) Hedda please . . .

LVBORG

Perhaps I prefer to stay and talk to you.

HEDDA

Bravo. (*To THEA*) You see? He sticks to his guns. He
won't be shaken. What on earth were you worried
about Thea? There was no need.

THEA

Worried?

HEDDA

When you came to me in such a state this morning.

THEA

Hedda, please!!

HEDDA

See for yourself. Look at him. There was no need to
get in a panic. Why were you so frightened?

LVBORG

What is all this?

THEA

Hedda, what are you doing?

HEDDA

The Judge has his eye on us again, dreadful man.

LVBORG

*(To THEA)* You were frightened?

THEA

*(To HEDDA)* How could you?

LVBORG

My loyal friend has no faith in me.

THEA

Eilert, please ...

LVBORG

*(Picks up a glass of punch)* Your health, Thea. *(He empties the glass, and refills it.)*

THEA

*(To HEDDA)* Why are you doing this?

LVBORG

Your health, Mrs Tesman. *(Lifts his glass)* Thank you for the information. To you. *(He drinks, and picks up the carafe again.)*

HEDDA

Steady. You're going to the Judge's party, don't forget.

THEA

No!

HEDDA

Be quiet. They can hear you.

LVBORG puts down his glass.

LVBORG

*(To THEA)* Does your husband know you're here?

THEA

Oh Hedda, you've broken my heart.

LVBORG

Did he tell you to follow me?

THEA

Eilert!

LVBORG

Here's to the Magistrate!

HEDDA

No more now. You're going to read your manuscript, remember?

LVBORG

(Puts down his glass, calmly to THEA) They'll see. Never mind what I was. That's over, thanks to you. I owe you everything.

THEA

And you won't go out.

BRACK and JORGEN enter from the back room.

LVBORG

(Rises) I'll join you if I may.

THEA

No, please! ...

HEDDA

(Grasps THEA'S arm) Sssh! ...

BRACK

You'll come?

LVBORG

Yes.

BRACK

Delighted.

JORGEN

Splendid. But how will Mrs Elvsted get home, Hedda?

HEDDA

Oh, don't worry about that.

LVBORG

I shall come and fetch her. At ten o'clock. Will that
suit, Mrs Elvsted?

HEDDA

We're obliged to you.

JORGEN

I hope you won't expect me back so soon, Hedda.

HEDDA

Stay as long as you want, my dear.

THEA

I'll wait then, Mr Lvborg. Till you come for me.

LVBORG

I shall be here.

BRACK

On with the party! Let's hope we'll have what a
certain beautiful lady suggests, a splendid night out.

HEDDA

A certain beautiful lady would adore to be present –
invisibly – just to hear and see all the antics.

BRACK

Oh, not at all a suitable occupation for beautiful
ladies.

JORGEN

(*Laughs*) I agree, what?

BRACK

Goodnight then, ladies.

LVBORG

(*Bows*) Until ten o'clock.

The MEN leave.

BERTA enters, sets down a lamp and goes. THEA walks up and down.

THEA

Oh Hedda, how is this going to end?

HEDDA

With Eilert Lvborg, joyful and triumphant, standing in front of me, with vine leaves in his hair.

THEA

Can you be sure of that?

HEDDA

He'll be himself. Freed ... released for the rest of his life. You'll see.

THEA

I pray to God you know what you're doing.

HEDDA

He'll come through. He must!

THEA

Hedda!

HEDDA

He must, that's all.

THEA

(*Slight pause*) What is it? What is it that you want?

HEDDA

For once it will be <u>my</u> influence.

THEA

Surely, you've enough influence already?

HEDDA

No.

THEA

Not over your husband?

HEDDA

Tesman?! I have nothing. I have nothing, and you are
rich, and I think, after all, I will burn off your hair . . .
Burn it all off!

THEA

Stop it! Hedda, let go, you're frightening me!

BERTA appears from the back room.

BERTA

I've laid out a tray on the table, madam, is that right?

HEDDA

Mrs Elvsted and I will come through.

BERTA

(*Going*) . . . come through . . .

BERTA exits.

THEA

No. I'd like to leave now.

HEDDA

There's no-one to take you.

**THEA**

I'll walk home alone. I'd like to go now, please.

**HEDDA**

Oh, don't be so stupid, you little fool. We'll wait together and at ten o'clock Eilert Lvborg will come through the door with vine leaves in his hair. Vine leaves, do you hear?

She pulls THEA into the back room.

*Fade to black.*

ACT THREE

The same scene, lamps low, curtains drawn. The door of the stove is open and the light from the fire visible.

THEA wrapped in a shawl, huddles by the fire. On the sofa HEDDA lies asleep, covered by a rug. THEA sits up, listens, and then lies back wearily.

THEA

(*Sighs*) Ohh ...

Silence. BERTA enters quietly with a letter.

THEA

(*Sits up*) Is he back?

BERTA

It's a letter, Miss. For Master Jorgie. Miss Tesman's new maid come over with it.

THEA

(*Alarmed*) In the middle of the night?

BERTA

Night? It's morning. Seven o'clock. (*She waves the letter.*)

THEA

Morning? Leave it on the table. We'll see he gets it.

BERTA

Gets it. Shall I see to the lamp? It's starting to smoke.

THEA

Thank you. Could you draw the curtains?

BERTA

The curtains.

BERTA turns out the lamp, then draws back the curtains.
Daylight floods in.

THEA

Daylight? And no-one's come in?

BERTA

Not a soul, Miss.

THEA

Mr Lvborg?

BERTA

Not a sight of him.

THEA

Oh dear.

BERTA

I've known that gentleman since he was a lad. They
shouldn't ought to have taken him. He didn't ought to
have gone with 'em.

THEA

Ssh! We mustn't wake Mrs Tesman.

BERTA

Ooh, sorry. (*Whispers*) Shall I make up the fire?

THEA

Oh, don't bother for me.

BERTA

Suit yourself, Miss.

She goes out. HEDDA wakes up.

HEDDA

Who was that?

THEA

Only the maid.

HEDDA

(*Sits up*) What time is it?

THEA

(*Looks at her watch*) Just after seven.

HEDDA

Seven? When did Tesman come in?

THEA

He isn't back yet. No-one is.

HEDDA

They've been out all night?

THEA

Yes.

HEDDA

We should have gone to bed. Did you get any sleep?

THEA

No.

HEDDA

Oh, for heavens' sake. Why didn't you make yourself comfortable?

THEA shakes her head, unable to answer.

HEDDA

What are you worried about?

THEA

Aren't you?

### HEDDA

Of course not. Obviously, the party went on into the small hours. Tesman was worried about waking us up in the middle of the night. Anyway, he probably preferred not to be seen in the state I've no doubt he was in.

### THEA

But where are they?

### HEDDA

He'll have gone to his aunts.

### THEA

No. They've just sent him a note. It's there on the table.

HEDDA crosses, picks up the letter, and inspects it.

### HEDDA

Ah, from the beloved Miss Tesman. He's obviously not there. Still with the Judge, I daresay. Having listened all night to Eilert, mesmerizing them.

### THEA

You don't believe that.

### HEDDA

Turning the pages, his eyes alive. Of course I believe it! Don't you, mere mortal? Oh, go to bed.

### THEA

What's the point? I won't be able to sleep.

### HEDDA

Yes, you will. Go up to my room and pull down the blinds.

THEA

I need to be here.

HEDDA

You _are_ here. I'll call you as soon as they arrive.

THEA

You promise to wake me?

HEDDA

(*Nods*) Of course. Go and get some rest.

THEA

Thank you.

THEA goes.

HEDDA crosses and looks out of the window. She picks up a hand mirror, tidies her hair and rings the bell.

BERTA

Did you want something, Madam?

HEDDA

Yes. Build up the fire, it's freezing in here.

BERTA

I'll soon get you warmed up.

She rakes the embers and throws on logs. The DOORBELL rings. She straightens up.

BERTA

Was that the doorbell?

HEDDA

Answer it. I'll see to the fire.

BERTA exits.

HEDDA kneels before the fire and puts on more wood.

JORGEN enters, looking white and serious. He makes to cross.

HEDDA

(*Without looking up*) Good morning.

JORGEN

(*Jumps*) Hedda! You're up!

HEDDA

You sound amazed.

JORGEN

I thought you would still be asleep.

HEDDA

I've given my bed to Mrs Elvsted, so I'd be obliged if
you'd tread quietly.

JORGEN

Mrs Elvsted? What is she doing here?

HEDDA

She's been here all night. No-one came to collect her.

She closes the stove and rises, wiping her hands.

HEDDA

So, did you have a splendid evening?

JORGEN

I hope you weren't worried.

HEDDA

Not in the least. I asked if you had enjoyed yourself.

JORGEN

Well, yes, it was. Anyway, early on. That was when
Eilert and I were able to retire and he read while the
Judge was otherwise engaged.

HEDDA

He read to you.

JORGEN

Just to me. It was ... it was ...

HEDDA

Tell me!

JORGEN

(*Simply*) I was overwhelmed, Hedda.

HEDDA

Overwhelmed?

JORGEN

I don't think it's ever been my privilege to listen
to anything so impressive. Impressive in scope, in
daring, in depth. The language itself! Just to have
been the first to listen is an honour that I doubt can
ever be repeated in my life. I was witness to a major,
innovative work that will certainly change the world.

HEDDA

Never mind the book. How is ... ?

JORGEN

And do you know what I felt? Hedda, I can honestly
say that I've never, ever, experienced such a feeling
before.

HEDDA

Feeling? What feeling?

JORGEN

Envy. I sat across from him, and I was invaded with
wave after wave of overwhelming ...

HEDDA

Envy.

JORGEN

There we were, and I looked at him, and all I could
think was – why? All that talent sitting inside the
head of a man so wild – profligate even . . .

HEDDA

A man not afraid to live.

JORGEN

Hedda, there are limits. To be divinely endowed with
a God-given gift carries responsibility. To watch it, as
I have, being thrown away. Treated as if nothing at
all.

HEDDA

What happened after he finished?

JORGEN

Well we all enjoyed ourselves, especially Eilert.

HEDDA

I daresay. Did he have vine leaves in his hair?

JORGEN

Vine leaves? (Laughs) I didn't see any. A lot of the
time he was talking about a woman. He went on and
on about her.

HEDDA

What woman?

JORGEN

I don't know. He just kept talking about her.

HEDDA

What did he say?

JORGEN

Apparently, she's his inspiration.

HEDDA

Inspiration?

JORGEN

He said the thought of her kept him alive. He must
mean Mrs Elvsted.

HEDDA

Little Thea? Hardly.

JORGEN

Who else is there?

HEDDA

I can't imagine. Where is he now?

JORGEN

Eilert? I don't know. Brack needed some fresh air,
so we agreed to take Eilert back to his lodgings. He
was ...

HEDDA

I daresay.

JORGEN

But then, Hedda ... I still can't ... (*He shakes his head
in disbelief.*)

HEDDA

What happened?

JORGEN

The others went on ahead. I was trying to catch up
when I tripped over something. You will never believe
me when I tell you what it was. What do you think?

HEDDA

How should I know?

JORGEN

This!

He pulls out a large wrapped package from his pocket.

JORGEN

Please – not a word to anyone.

HEDDA

What is it?

JORGEN

Eilert's book! His precious, irreplaceable manuscript.
He dropped it in the street without even noticing! Can
you imagine?

HEDDA

Why didn't you give it back?

JORGEN

In his state, how could I?

HEDDA moves away.

HEDDA

Who else knows?

JORGEN

No-one.

HEDDA

Only you.

JORGEN

Yes. And you mustn't say a word. For his sake.

HEDDA

Did you tell him you had it?

JORGEN

I didn't get a chance. He went off with the others.

HEDDA

They took him home?

JORGEN

Presumably. Brack disappeared, and then I ...

HEDDA

Yes, what about you?

JORGEN

The rest of us went off to find a coffee house. Believe
me, we needed it.

HEDDA

(Abstracted) Ye-es ...

JORGEN

I'll go to bed now. Give Eilert a chance to sleep it off.
And then take the manuscript round to him. Put his
mind at rest. Of course, he may not even know that
it's missing.

He clasps the manuscript protectively. HEDDA lies back on the
sofa, and lifts a hand.

HEDDA

Give it to me. I'd like to read it.

JORGEN

Oh, not now surely Hedda? I really can't let it out of
my hands.

HEDDA

Why not?

JORGEN

I must get it back to him. He'll be distraught. It's the
only copy. Suppose it went astray?

HEDDA

Then he'd have to write it all over again.

JORGEN

No, no, no. Impossible. A work of imagination can't be
replicated.

HEDDA

Can it not?

JORGEN

No.

HEDDA

If you say so. By the way, there's a letter for you. (*She
indicates.*)

JORGEN crosses, picks up the letter, and reads.

JORGEN

Oh Hedda!

HEDDA

What?

JORGEN

It's Aunt Rina.

HEDDA

Dead?

JORGEN

No, but in a very bad way. I must go over at once. (*He
moves, turns back.*) Hedda?

HEDDA

Yes?

JORGEN

Would you ... could you bring yourself to come with
me?

HEDDA

Out of the question. I want nothing to do with illness –
people dying. How can you ask? You know I hate
anything ugly. I won't have it.

JORGEN

I'm sorry. I forgot. I beg your pardon.

HEDDA

You'd better get off.

JORGEN

Yes, I must dash. What did I do with my coat!

JORGEN exits, and returns – putting on his coat.

JORGEN

I'll ... I'll go then.

BERTA enters, and whispers in HEDDA's ear.

BERTA

It's the Judge. He'd like a word, Mum.

JORGEN

At this hour? No. Yes. No, tell him I can't just now.

HEDDA

Ask him to come in.

BERTA goes.

JORGEN

(Whispers) Hedda. The manuscript!

HEDDA grabs it from the footstool. JORGEN holds out his hand.

JORGEN

Thank you ...

HEDDA

No. I'll take care of it for now.

She puts the package away in one of the drawers of the writing table.

BERTA ushers in BRACK.

BERTA

Judge Brack, Madam.

BERTA bobs to the JUDGE, then to HEDDA. She decides not to bob to JORGEN, and exits.

HEDDA

An unusually early bird. Anything amiss?

BRACK

No, no. Are you off, Tesman?

JORGEN

Aunt Rina's been taken ill. I'm afraid it's serious this time.

BRACK

Then you'd better hurry, man.

JORGEN

Yes, I must. (*He attempts to kiss HEDDA.*) Goodbye.

He goes. HEDDA settles on the sofa.

HEDDA

Tea?

BRACK

Perhaps later.

HEDDA

I hear you had a good evening last night.

BRACK

Why, what has he been telling you?

HEDDA

Nothing. Except that he went off to a coffee house to sober up. Were you ... ?

BRACK

I wasn't with them.

HEDDA

I gather Eilert was delivered back safely.

BRACK

Tesman said that?

HEDDA

So he was told.

BRACK

A simple soul, Jorgen.

HEDDA

True. What is the matter? Is something up?

BRACK

I'm afraid so.

HEDDA

That's why you're here? Do sit ... Well?

BRACK

Some of my guests went on to another establishment after they left me.

HEDDA

Eilert?

BRACK

He said no at first.

HEDDA

But then?

BRACK

He became, as it were, somewhat inspired. Bacchus
replaced Apollo. Men may worship virtue but, alas,
not always.

HEDDA

Oh, I don't see your descending into the less than
divine, Judge. What happened?

BRACK

Do you know of a woman called Madame Diane? She
runs an establishment for . . . entertainment.

HEDDA

Red-haired? A singer?

BRACK

Among other things. Lvborg knew her in the old days.
I believe he was her most ardent patron at one time.

HEDDA

So, the evening went well?

BRACK

Not entirely. What began as a renewal of
acquaintance ended, I'm afraid to say, in a brawl.
There was an argument over money. In the end, the
police were called. Lvborg, I fear, is in trouble.

HEDDA

Trouble?

BRACK

Apparently, he was in, what shall we say, a combative
mood. He decided to take on the police force. Which
was unwise. He was arrested.

HEDDA

You saw all this?

BRACK

(Shakes his head) No. I was informed of it by the
police.

HEDDA

Alas for the vine leaves ...

BRACK

I'm sorry?

HEDDA

Well, you've no cause for concern. You weren't
involved.

BRACK

I was his host earlier in the evening. When that fact is
read out in court ...

HEDDA

In court? Will it come to that?

BRACK

Undoubtedly.

HEDDA

It hardly concerns Tesman or me.

BRACK

He may attempt to use you.

HEDDA

How?

BRACK

You must be aware of the situation with Mrs Elvsted.
That she does not intend to return to her husband.

HEDDA

That is no concern of mine.

BRACK

But it might be. After last night's adventures, most
doors will be closed to Mr Lvborg.

HEDDA

So mine should be too?

BRACK

It would be wise. And, I confess, the inconvenience of
an intruder into our ... friendship ...

HEDDA

As cock of the walk, you would seek to ...

BRACK

To defend my position. With vigour.

HEDDA

I see. You're a dangerous man, Judge.

BRACK

You think so?

HEDDA

It's as well that I've nothing to fear from you.

BRACK

Have you not?

HEDDA

Nothing that I can think of.

BRACK

(*Laughs*) Who knows? Who knows, Mrs Hedda?

HEDDA

Is that a threat?

BRACK

(*Rises*) On the contrary. My sacred aim is the protection of our 'arrangement.' A worthy crusade, wouldn't you say?

HEDDA

(*Sarcastic.*) Celestial.

BRACK

Well, I've delivered my message. I must be on my way. Good-day to you, Mrs Hedda.

He crosses to the French windows.

HEDDA

(*Rising*) You're going out by the garden?

BRACK

With your permission. A back way can be so intriguing, don't you agree?

HEDDA

Even with the risk of being shot?

BRACK

Oh, people don't shoot sitting birds. A tame cock can be a valued species. A useful household addition.

They laugh.

BRACK bows and goes.

HEDDA watches him, then crosses to the writing desk. She takes
out the package and removes Lvborg's book.

BERTA

(Offstage) No, you can't come in. It's not convenient.
She's not at home!

LVBORG erupts into the room, followed by BERTA.

LVBORG

Get out of my way.

HEDDA puts the book away swiftly.

BERTA

Madam, he just pushed . . .

HEDDA

That's all right. (She waves BERTA off.)

BERTA exits. Silence. Then LVBORG bows.

HEDDA

A little late to be collecting Mrs Elvsted, wouldn't you
say?

LVBORG

Is she still here? Where's Tesman?

HEDDA

In bed.

LVBORG

When did he come in?

HEDDA

Half an hour ago. I gather the party was a success.

LVBORG

Did he say anything?

HEDDA

He may have. I don't remember. I was half asleep.

THEA enters. She runs towards LVBORG.

THEA

Oh Eilert. Oh, you're here!

She tries to embrace him, but he turns away.

THEA

What's the matter? What's happened?

LVBORG

It's over.

THEA

What?

LVBORG

I'm finished.

THEA

Don't say that.

LVBORG

You'll say it when you hear what ...

THEA

No. I don't want to know what happened last night.

LVBORG

I'm not talking about last night.

THEA

Then what?

LVBORG

It's over. You and me. Finished.

THEA

Why?

He shakes his head.

THEA

How can you say that?

He walks away.

THEA

I've been of use to you, haven't I? For the work?

LVBORG

There won't be any more work.

THEA

Then my life is over.

LVBORG

Forget me. Forget you ever knew me.

THEA

You know I can't do that!

LVBORG

Go home, Thea.

THEA

No. I'm staying. Here, with you. Till the new book comes out.

He sits abruptly, his head in his hands.

THEA

I want to see you honoured, and respected, for what you are. I want to be there – witness your triumph. The glory of the book's achievement.

LVBORG

There won't be any book.

THEA

Why not? Of course there will!

LVBORG

There is no book.

THEA

Eilert. What have you done? Where is it? Where is the manuscript? Where is it? I have a right to know.

LVBORG

There is no manuscript. I've torn it up.

THEA

(*Screams*) No! No! No!

HEDDA

You've destroyed it?

LVBORG

Don't you believe me?

HEDDA

Of course, if you say so. You've torn up your manuscript.

THEA

Oh, my God. All that thought, all that work, all that life!

LVBORG

Yes. Life. Thrown away, smashed.

THEA

When?

LVBORG

Last night. A thousand pieces into the fjord. Gone.
Finished. Like me.

THEA

You've killed our child.

LVBORG

Yes. That's what I've done. That's exactly what I've
done.

THEA

It was my child too!

HEDDA

(*Turns away*) Child ...

THEA weeps. They wait silently until she stops.

THEA

It's over then.

She rises, crosses, and puts on her coat.

HEDDA

Where will you go?

THEA

I don't know.

She looks across at LVBORG. He regards her bleakly.

THEA turns and goes.

HEDDA

Can't you take her home?

LVBORG

And let people see her with me?

HEDDA

Why not? I don't know what went on last night, but it
can't have been that bad, surely?

LVBORG

*(Pause)* She was the one who made it happen. She
created the book, not me. It was her will. Her energy.

HEDDA

*(To herself)* Little Thea? Little Thea?! *(She crosses
and stands over him.)* You're being very heartless in
that case – after all she's done for you.

LVBORG

*(Mutters)* Oh, she's done for me. *(Short pause)* I lied
to her.

HEDDA

Lied?

LVBORG

It's not at the bottom of the fjord.

HEDDA

The book? So, where is it?

LVBORG

Who knows? *(He lifts his head laughing)* "I do
apologise, I appear to have mislaid our son. He's out
there somewhere. Alive. Dead. Who knows? Will you
ever see him again? Unlikely." All that time, she ...
Waylaying. Beguiling. Finding discipline where there
was none. *(He walks about.)* Such a mild woman. A
face in the crowd. Unexciting. But she's finished me.

HEDDA

Finished you?

LVBORG

There's nothing left. I'm used up. She's used me up.

HEDDA

(*Pause*) So it's over. What are you going to do?

LVBORG

Why do you think I'm here?

Pause.

HEDDA crosses, takes out one of her pistols, and hands it to him.

LVBORG

Thank you.

HEDDA

I nearly killed you with this once.

He puts it in his pocket.

HEDDA

Don't come here again.

They look at each other. He turns to go.

HEDDA

(*Calls*) Do it beautifully.

LVBORG pauses. And goes.

HEDDA crosses to the window to watch him go. She stands for a long moment. then begins to walk up and down, arms clasped. She pauses, then resumes walking. Only now, she moves more and more quickly until, suddenly, she darts across the room, wrenches open the drawer and takes out the manuscript.

She holds it, then rips open the packaging. She looks at the bound manuscript, and riffles the pages. She walks back and forth, reading.

Then she stands, clasping the manuscript to her.

Dreamily, she crosses and sits by the fire, clutching the manuscript.

Absently, she leans forward, and opens the stove. And stays, nursing the manuscript, for a long time. Then she throws it in the fire in one violent gesture.

HEDDA

There goes the child.

She sits back, watching the flames.

HEDDA

Thea, did you know your hair was on fire?

*Fade to black.*

# ACT FOUR

The Drawing Room. Evening.

HEDDA moves slowly back and forth. She goes into the back room.

Loud Wagnerian discords on the piano are heard.

As she returns, BERTA enters with a lamp. She is dressed in black with black ribbons in her cap, and her face shows signs of weeping.

HEDDA crosses to the French windows and looks out.

As she moves away from the window, BERTA bobs and draws the curtains.

She bobs again and exits.

Pause. The sound of VOICES.

Enter MISS TESMAN, from the hall, in black hat and veiling.

HEDDA crosses to greet her, extending her hand.

> MISS TESMAN
> Well, Hedda. As you see, my dear sister's struggles
> are over at last.

> HEDDA
> Tesman sent me a note.

> MISS TESMAN
> He promised he would, but I had to tell you myself.

Bring the sad news of death into this house of life.

> HEDDA
> Thank you, that was kind.

MISS TESMAN

Why did she have to leave us now? Now is not the time for this house to be in mourning. Now is a time for joy – expectation.

HEDDA

(*Cuts across*) I believe she died peacefully.

MISS TESMAN

Yes, it was an easy death. She was able to see her dear Jorgie for one last time. She went quietly after that. Is Jorgen back yet?

HEDDA

Not as far as I'm aware. Do sit down.

MISS TESMAN

Thank you no, Hedda dear. I must go home and lay her out. Make sure she looks beautiful for her last journey.

HEDDA

Can I do anything? I mean ...

MISS TESMAN

Heavens no. You mustn't concern yourself, especially just now. We can't have you thinking about death and mourning. That wouldn't do at all. It's the way of the world. A shroud today, but another sort of sewing in this house soon, thanks be to God.

JORGEN enters.

HEDDA

There you are.

JORGEN

Aunt Julla! You're here, with Hedda. Well!

MISS TESMAN

I'm just going, dear boy. Did you manage to do
everything I asked?

JORGEN

I'm afraid not. My head is in a spin. I'll come over
later when I'm more myself.

MISS TESMAN

Oh, Jorgie dear, you mustn't take it so badly.
Remember. In the midst of sorrow, we are in joy. Keep
a glad heart. Be joyous, as I am.

JORGEN

About losing Aunt Rina?

HEDDA

You'll miss her, Miss Tesman.

MISS TESMAN

Oh yes. For a little while, but dear Rina's place will be
filled soon enough. Her room won't be empty for long.

JORGEN

You've arranged for someone else already?

HEDDA stifles a laugh.

MISS TESMAN

Not yet, but the world is full of lonely souls, Jorgie,
take my word for it. There will be some poor invalid
out there who needs nursing.

HEDDA

Another incumbrance?

MISS TESMAN

Incumbrance? Caring for Rina has been no cross for
me!

HEDDA

She was your sister. It's hardly the same – a stranger
in the house.

MISS TESMAN

The sick are so grateful. And I must make myself
useful – find something to live for. Mind you, an old
aunt can be a boon when needed, as you'll find out
soon enough.

HEDDA

I beg your pardon?

JORGEN

(*Uneasy*) Everything will sort itself out, what?

MISS TESMAN

I'll be on my way. Something tells me you two have
things to talk about. (*Smiles*) Who knows, Jorgie?
Perhaps Hedda has a little secret for you? Goodbye,
I must get back to Rina. (*She turns back in the
doorway.*) Dear God, isn't it strange? Rina is at peace.
As I am. She's with your father, our beloved brother.
Both gone, yet still here in my heart.

JORGEN

Of course, they are. Where they belong.

MISS TESMAN goes. HEDDA surveys JORGEN coldly.

HEDDA

You seem more upset than she is.

JORGEN

About Aunt Rina? Of course, but it <u>was</u> expected. It's
the other thing. Eilert.

HEDDA

Where is he? Have you spoken to him?

JORGEN

I went straight to his lodgings, to say that his
manuscript was safe.

HEDDA

No doubt he was relieved.

JORGEN

He wasn't there. I spoke to Mrs Elvsted. She said
Eilert had come here this morning. Did he?

HEDDA

Yes, he arrived just after you left.

JORGEN

And? Apparently, he's going about telling everyone
he's torn up the manuscript. What did he say to you?

HEDDA

The same. He said it was no longer in existence. That
he'd torn it up.

JORGEN

Mad! (*A dreadful thought strikes him.*) You didn't
give it to him?

HEDDA

No.

JORGEN

Did you tell him we had it?

HEDDA

No. Did you tell Thea where it was?

JORGEN

Given the circumstances between them, I thought it
better not to. But perhaps you should have told him,
Hedda? He's in a dreadful state. We don't know what
he might do. I must get over there right away. Where
is it?

HEDDA

What?

JORGEN

The manuscript!

HEDDA

I haven't got it.

JORGEN

What do you mean, you haven't got it? Why not?

HEDDA

I burned it.

JORGEN

(*Screams*) Burned it? You burned it? Eilert's
manuscript? His book?

HEDDA

For God's sake, keep your voice down.

JORGEN

Burned it? No. You can't have! It's not possible!

HEDDA crosses, opens the fire and displays the ashes.

JORGEN

What have you done? What have you done? You have
destroyed someone else's property. That is against
the law. Ask Judge Brack.

HEDDA

I suggest that you say nothing, either to Judge Brack
or anyone else.

JORGEN

But to ... ? How could you do anything so ... it's
unbelievable! What on earth came over you? Are you
not yourself? Tell me, I need to know!

HEDDA

(Pause) I did it for you.

JORGEN

For me?!

HEDDA

You came back here this morning and told me that
he had been reading to you. That what you heard
was magnificent, better than anything you could
ever imagine, ever dream of doing yourself. You were
jealous. You said so.

JORGEN

I know I did. It's simply that I was surprised to feel
such ... such ...

HEDDA

Envy.

JORGEN

I didn't mean it. Not seriously.

HEDDA

You said you were jealous, Jorgen.

JORGEN gasps.

HEDDA

I couldn't bear it for you. I couldn't bear to see you pushed aside.

JORGEN

You called me Jorgen. (*In amazement*) You did it for me! My God, Hedda, do you really mean you feel that deeply for me? I never knew!

HEDDA

Then you should know. Especially now. I have some news for you. (*But she cannot bring herself to say it.*) Oh, ask your Aunt.

JORGEN

Oh, my dear love. Do you mean ... Are you telling me? Oh, can it be possible? Already?

HEDDA

Shut up – the servant will hear you.

JORGEN

The servant? You mean Berta? I must go and tell her at once!

HEDDA

No.

JORGEN

No?

HEDDA

Don't. I can't.

JORGEN

Dearest, what is it? Surely? Aren't you ... ? I'm so happy, I want to rush out and tell everyone. But, if you'd rather I didn't. I won't say anything to Berta.

### HEDDA

Why not tell everyone? Tell the world. Every earthly
inhabitant from here to Vladivostok.

### JORGEN

Perhaps Aunt Ju. Yes, Aunt Ju must know. Oh, and
Hedda, I must tell her that you called me Jorgen for
the first time. It will make her so happy.

### HEDDA

And that I burned Eilert Lvborg's manuscript for you.
Do you think she'll appreciate that?

### JORGEN

(*Remembering*) Oh heavens! What can we … ? We'd
better … Perhaps, for now, no-one should know. That
you would do that for me! I must certainly let Aunt
Julla know of your loyalty, your feelings for me. Is it
general, such attachment between husband and wife?

### HEDDA

Ask her. I'm sure she'll know.

### JORGEN

I will, at the right moment. But oh! Thinking about it.
Dreadful. The manuscript. Poor Eilert!

A KNOCK.

THEA enters.

### THEA

Hedda, good morning. May I come in? Do forgive me
for intruding.

### HEDDA

Why Thea, what's the matter?

JORGEN

Is it to do with Eilert?

THEA

Forgive me, but I am out of my mind with worry.

HEDDA

What about?

THEA

I am so afraid that he may have had an accident.

JORGEN

An accident? Eilert?

HEDDA

Well, has he? Has he, or hasn't he?

THEA

I don't know. When I got back to the boarding house
they were talking about him. The whole town is full of
the most awful rumours.

JORGEN

Take no notice. I can tell you, he went straight home
to bed.

HEDDA

What rumours? What were they saying?

THEA

I don't know! People went quiet when I said his name.
I didn't know what to do. I was too afraid to ask.

JORGEN

I'm sure there's nothing to worry about.

THEA

No. I heard Eilert's name. They mentioned the
hospital.

JORGEN

Hospital?

THEA

I was so frightened, I went straight to his rooms.

HEDDA

Was that wise?

THEA

What else could I do? I couldn't bear not knowing.

JORGEN

And you weren't able to find him?

THEA

*(Shakes her head)* They said he hadn't been home
since yesterday.

JORGEN

Yesterday?

THEA

Something's happened. I know it.

JORGEN

Perhaps I should go into town, try to find out?

HEDDA

No. Don't involve yourself.

BERTA ushers in JUDGE BRACK. His manner is serious. He nods,
greeting them silently.

JORGEN

My dear Judge . . .

BRACK

I felt obliged to call.

JORGEN

You've heard about Aunt Rina.

BRACK

Oh – yes.

JORGEN

Very sad.

BRACK

Indeed. A release nonetheless.

JORGEN

Was there something else? Has something else
happened?

HEDDA

Not more bad news?

BRACK

That would depend on how you look at it, Mrs Tesman.

THEA

It's to do with Eilert, isn't it?

BRACK

(*Looks at her intently*) What makes you say that, Mrs
Elvsted? Have you heard something?

JORGEN

For God's sake, Judge, tell us!

BRACK

I'm sorry. Bad news. He's been taken to the hospital.

HEDDA

Hospital?

THEA

(*Whispers*) Eilert ...

BRACK

I'm afraid he's dying.

THEA

(*Whispers*) No ...

HEDDA

Already?

THEA

Oh Hedda! (*Weeps.*) Hedda! And we parted so ... with such ...

HEDDA

(*Whispers*) Thea, be quiet!

THEA

(*Takes no notice*) I have to go to him. I must go. Now!

BRACK

I'm sorry. They won't let you in.

THEA

But what happened? What's happened to him?

JORGEN

He hasn't tried to harm himself?

HEDDA

Why not, if he wants to?

JORGEN

Hedda, how can you!

BRACK

(*Watching HEDDA steadily*) I'm afraid that Mrs Tesman is right.

THEA

Oh please . . .

JORGEN

You're saying he tried to commit suicide? No, I can't believe it. Tried to kill himself?

HEDDA

With a pistol.

BRACK

Well guessed again, Mrs Tesman.

THEA

(*Trying to compose herself*) When did this happen, Judge?

BRACK

Between three and four this afternoon.

JORGEN

My God, where?

BRACK

No idea, my dear chap. In his lodgings I suppose,

THEA

No. I was there.

BRACK

Somewhere else then. I don't know. I was simply told that he had shot himself in the chest.

HEDDA

In the chest? Not a head shot?

BRACK

Through the chest, Mrs Tesman.

HEDDA

Through the chest. That would do.

BRACK

Why, Mrs Tesman?

HEDDA

Why not?

THEA

And you're saying the wound is fatal?

BRACK

Absolutely. He may well be dead already.

THEA

Yes. I feel it.

JORGEN

Where did you learn all this?

BRACK

From the police.

HEDDA

It's done. Oh, the beauty of it!

BRACK

Mrs Tesman!

THEA

Beauty? In killing yourself?

JORGEN

How can there possibly be beauty in such as this?!

HEDDA

Eilert Lvborg has done what he had to do. What he
had the courage to do.

THEA

No! He was out of his mind.

HEDDA

You're wrong. Quite wrong.

THEA

Of course, he was out of his mind. He must have been,
to tear up his manuscript.

BRACK

His manuscript? You mean he destroyed it?

THEA

Yes. He told me.

JORGEN

(*Pulls HEDDA aside*) This is going to haunt us forever.

BRACK

I see. Very odd.

JORGEN, agitated, walks up and down.

JORGEN

It's unbearable, the thought of losing him. Not only
that – losing his work, the wonderful, wonderful book
that would have made him immortal!

THEA

Yes. If only one could ... if there was some way ...

JORGEN

What?

THEA

To piece it together again.

JORGEN

God, yes. Oh, dear Lord, I'd give anything ...

THEA

(*Quietly*) It may not be impossible, Mr Tesman.

JORGEN

How?!

THEA

I have all his notes. The notes he dictated to me.

HEDDA

(*Groans*) Ah!!

JORGEN

You kept them? You've got them, Mrs Elvsted?

THEA

I brought them away with me when I left home. I've been carrying them with me for safety ever since I arrived.

JORGEN

May I see?

THEA picks up and unlatches her leather bag. She takes out two heavy folders.

THEA

They are not in order, I'm afraid.

JORGEN

Oh, that can be sorted out. If we were to work together – a joint effort – with my experience and your familiarity with text.

THEA

Could we? Would it be possible?

JORGEN

I don't see why not. If the notes are full enough.

THEA

Oh, they are! I took down every word!

JORGEN

Then it may be possible to reassemble the material ...

THEA

... put the chapters together ...

JORGEN

If, as you say, the material is extant.

BRACK

Bravo.

JORGEN

Hedda! It sounds as if the book will live after all. Isn't that splendid? Under the circumstances, can one do less?

HEDDA walks away.

BRACK

A joint effort ... under your names ...

JORGEN

No, no!

THEA

No, no, no. His work. Under his name.

JORGEN

Eilert's work entirely. Mrs Thea and I may perhaps permit ourselves to append a foreword ... and reference notes of course. (*To THEA*) Can it be achieved?

THEA

Yes – we must!

JORGEN

It shall be done. I'll stake my life on it.

HEDDA

Your life?

JORGEN

Every free moment from this day forth. My book will
have to wait, Hedda. This is more important. I'm sure
you understand. I owe it to Eilert.

HEDDA

If you say so.

JORGEN

We must be strong, Mrs Elvsted. Something good
shall come out of this tragedy. We have it in our
power. Will you join me? (*He indicates the back
room.*) Do you think you could manage to ... Shall we
try to be useful at this awful time?

THEA

Yes. Oh yes, Mr Tesman!

JORGEN

(*He escorts her to the other room.*) We can at least
begin to organise our thoughts.

THEA

Indeed!

They go into the back room, and sit across from each other, heads
down, immersing themselves in the notes.

HEDDA crosses to the stove and sits. BRACK rises and joins her.

HEDDA

Such an act.

BRACK

Lvborg?

HEDDA

The release of it!

BRACK

For him?

HEDDA

For me. To know there is still someone in this world
worthy of Olympus.

BRACK

My dear Hedda.

HEDDA

Surely you can understand the supremacy of a single
superb act.

BRACK

He has obviously been close to you. Very close.

HEDDA

Not your concern. All I know is that Eilert Lvborg had
the courage to live – and to die. The courage to choose
for himself. To live celestially, and to die by his own
choice. Beautifully.

BRACK

Is that what you believe?

HEDDA

I am witness to it.

BRACK

Then I am sorry to have to spoil your charming fairy
tale.

                    HEDDA

Fairy tale?

                    BRACK

Oh, what's the difference? Your illusions will be
shattered soon enough. You may as well know the
truth.

                    HEDDA

Know what?

                    BRACK

That he didn't shoot himself. Not purposely.

                    HEDDA

What?!

                    BRACK

The facts of this mess are not exactly as I reported
them just now.

                    HEDDA

What? What haven't you said?

                    BRACK

I omitted certain details. To spare the feelings of Mrs
Elvsted.

                    HEDDA

What details?

                    BRACK

In the first place, he is already dead.

                    HEDDA

I know that.

BRACK

At the hospital. He died without regaining consciousness. And it didn't happen at his lodgings.

HEDDA

What difference does that make?

BRACK

He was removed, after the shooting, from the bedroom of Madame Diane.

HEDDA

(*Half rises and sits.*) That's impossible. He could not have been there today.

BRACK

It was a return visit. To retrieve something that he said had been stolen from him. Apparently, he was out of his mind. Raving about a lost child ...

HEDDA

Child?

BRACK

His manuscript, I presumed. But now I hear he'd already destroyed that, so it must have been something else. His wallet perhaps.

HEDDA

And you say that is where he was found?

BRACK

Yes. With a pistol which had been discharged and which had killed him instantly.

HEDDA

Through the heart.

BRACK

No. Through the groin. Through the groin, Hedda.

HEDDA rises, and paces.

HEDDA

Why? Why this life-sentence of mind-poisoning
banality? (*She paces.*) Why?

BRACK

There is another matter.

HEDDA

(*Snarls*) Naturally even more debased.

BRACK

Not necessarily. A possible ... inconvenience.

HEDDA

Inconvenience? To you?

BRACK

The pistol Lvborg was carrying ...

HEDDA

What about it?

BRACK

It was, I presume, stolen.

HEDDA

No.

BRACK

No? He didn't steal it?

HEDDA

No.

JORGEN and THEA enter from the back room. BRACK puts a finger
to his lips.

JORGEN

It's very dark in there, Hedda. May we use your writing-table?

HEDDA

Of course. I'll move my papers.

JORGEN

Don't worry, there's plenty of room.

HEDDA

Allow me.

HEDDA picks up an object covered with music sheets, adds more covering, and removes it to the back room. JORGEN sets out papers on the writing-table, brings over a lamp, and he and THEA settle down to work.

HEDDA returns and stands behind THEA, ruffling her hair.

HEDDA

Well, pretty little Thea, a new quest. The Lvborg memorial!

THEA

(*Looks up*) It won't be easy.

JORGEN

We'll manage. We must. With my experience, and

Mrs Elvsted's excellent groundwork, we'll make a splendid team.

He pats THEA's hand. They smile at each other and settle down with the papers.

HEDDA crosses, and sits on a stool by the fire. BRACK stands over her, leaning on the armchair.

HEDDA

(*Low*) What were you saying? About the pistol.

BRACK

Saying? I was saying that he must have stolen it.

HEDDA

What makes you think that?

BRACK

Because there's no other explanation. (*Silence.*) He was here this morning, was he not?

HEDDA

Yes.

BRACK

Were you alone with him?

HEDDA

For a moment.

BRACK

Did you go out of the room while he was here?

HEDDA

Possibly.

BRACK

And where were your pistols at this time?

HEDDA

On the writing-table.

BRACK

Have you looked to see if they are still there?

HEDDA

No.

BRACK

I saw the pistol he had with him. I know it well.

HEDDA

Where is it? Have you got it?

BRACK

No. It's with the police.

HEDDA

What will they do?

BRACK

Trace the owner.

HEDDA

Will they succeed?

BRACK

(*Bends over, close.*) Not if I keep my mouth shut.

HEDDA

And if you don't?

BRACK

Then you must say that the pistol was stolen from
you.

HEDDA

I'd rather die first!

BRACK

Oh, people say such things. They never do them.

HEDDA

If the owner of the pistol became known ...

BRACK

If the owner of the pistol became known, there would
be one hell of a scandal. Your worst nightmare,
Hedda. Forced to descend into the arena with the

rest of humanity. You and Madame Diane, together in court.

She will be required to say whether the death was suicide. An accident. Or murder. Was he threatening her with the pistol? Did it go off accidentally? Or did she wrench it from him? Kill him, and then put it back in his pocket. A possibility. She's a resourceful woman.

> HEDDA
>
> All of which has nothing to do with me.

> BRACK
>
> You will be asked if you provided Lvborg with the gun.

If so, why? People will want to know.

HEDDA lowers her head.

> BRACK
>
> However. (*She looks up.*) There is no danger of that, so long as I don't say anything.

> HEDDA
>
> How can I be sure that you won't?

> BRACK
>
> Because I am a man of discretion.

> HEDDA
>
> Which puts you in the driving seat.

> BRACK
>
> Hedda!

> HEDDA
>
> You hold the cards, do you not?

She rises, and walks.

HEDDA

In return for your silence, I am to be dependent on
your ... interests.

BRACK

I anticipate that our ... interests ... will be mutual.

HEDDA

Nonetheless, I shan't be free.

BRACK

Oh, we resign ourselves to the inevitable in the end.

HEDDA

Do we?

She crosses to the writing-table, and leans over JORGEN.

HEDDA

Going well? That's good.

JORGEN

It will take months, I'm afraid – longer.

HEDDA

(Imitating him) "Well! Imagine that! Splendid!" (She
runs her hands through THEA's hair, dislodging its
neatness.) Strange, hmm? Who would have thought
it? Here you are, Thea, sitting with my husband, just
as you sat with Eilert.

THEA

Oh Hedda, if only I can inspire and support him in the
same way!

HEDDA

I'm sure you will.

JORGEN

Yes! You know, Hedda, I'm beginning to feel full of life
already. Something wonderful is happening here.

HEDDA

Can I be of use to either of you?

JORGEN

No, no, you're interrupting. Go back and talk to the
Judge. *(Calls)* I must depend on you to amuse Hedda
from now on, Brack.

BRACK

My pleasure. *(He rises, indicates a seat.)* Mrs
Tesman?

HEDDA

*(Regards him steadily)* Thank you.

She makes as if to sit, but changes her mind.

HEDDA

Would you forgive me, I'm feeling ... I'll take a rest on
the sofa.

JORGEN

*(Calls without looking up)* You do that, my dear.

HEDDA looks around at them. She crosses to the back room, and
draws the curtains behind her. Pause, then the CRASHING OF
CHORDS on the piano, making THEA jump.

THEA

Oh, good heavens!

JORGEN

*(Rises, calls)* Hedda, my dear! No music tonight
please. Think of Aunt Rina!

THEA whispers to him.

### JORGEN

... and poor Eilert!

HEDDA opens the curtains and surveys the room.

### HEDDA

Oh, I'll be quiet!

She closes the curtains. JORGEN returns to the writing-table.

### JORGEN

I daresay it's upsetting, having to watch us at this sad business. I say, I've had an idea. Why not, Mrs Elvsted – why not move in with Aunt Julla? You would be more than welcome. She will be grateful for the company in her loss. And I'll run over every day and we'll work together.

### THEA

Yes. Yes indeed, that might be the best for everyone.

### HEDDA

(*Calls*) I can hear you, Tesman. What am I to do, alone every day in this outpost? How do you suggest I pass the time?

### JORGEN

(*Busy with THEA at the notes, calls*) Judge Brack can look in on you. Yes Judge?

### BRACK

Every evening without fail.

### HEDDA

(*Calls clearly*) That will suit you, won't it Judge? Cock of the walk! Enjoy it!

Pause.

A SHOT from the back room.

THEA and JORGEN jolt to their feet.

JORGEN

Oh no! She's playing with those wretched pistols
again!

He dashes, and pulls back the curtains.

HEDDA is on the floor, her rear in the air, showing her underwear,
sprawled grotesquely in death.

JORGEN

(*Screams*) She's shot herself! She's blown her brains
out! Shot. (*Stunned.*) Imagine that. Imagine. Imagine
that, what? She's shot herself.

BRACK sits rigid in his chair.

BRACK

Shot herself? My God. People don't do that sort of
thing.

*Fade to black.*

The End.

# AFTER BIRTHDAY

for Carole Harrison

AFTER BIRTHDAY was first presented on the 5th of March, 1973, by *Inter-Action* and the *Women's Theatre Group* at the Almost Free Theatre, starring SHEILA KELLEY, and directed by PEDR JAMES.

Stage Manager                                     NICK BURGE

ASM                                     LAUREL-JANA MARKS

Lighting Design                                     PETER SOUTHCOTT

In 1979, AFTER BIRTHDAY was revived by the King's Head Theatre, Islington, where it ran from April 23rd to May 5th, starring CAROLE HARRISON, directed by SUE PARRISH.

Stage Manager                                     PHILIPPA MOUNTAIN

It is rare that one goes to a lunchtime and is confronted with a combination of equally high standard of writing, production and performance. Pam Gems's play, directed by Sue Parrish, achieves this rare distinction. It is a superb, powerful, disturbing presentation.

... Carole Harrison sensitively portrays a disturbed young woman waiting to be examined by an institution doctor. The writing is naturalistic, jerky stream-of-consciousness. Slowly, a background and narrative emerges, and character develops, through disjointed but methodical revelation – exposing a horrific, convoluted series of events.

YORI KOHUT. *The Stage* 03/05/1979

# AFTER BIRTHDAY



The waiting room of a prison hospital wing.

SANDRA, a working-class girl of twenty-two, is sitting on a plastic chair.

### SANDRA

Is somebody in there with him? I said … is somebody
in there with him? (*Pause.*) Can you talk in here?

There is no response.

SANDRA looks about, her eyes raking the audience as if they constitute her fellow prisoners. Her face hardens a little.

She reaches inside her clothes, takes out a cigarette, and a box of matches, lights up and draws needfully.

### SANDRA

You're not allowed to smoke, you know.

She draws again, sucking in the smoke, and expelling forcefully.

### SANDRA

Against the rules. Well, shall we have a sing-song? We
could all have a wank.

She grins round wolfishly. Then the smile dies on her face.

### SANDRA

I had it on a bus once. With a shvartzer. Had it forty-
five times one night. With thirty-five Algerians. Me
record, that. Hands up anybody who's never 'ad it?

She looks around, as if for a head count, and then grins cheerfully.

SANDRA

Well, that's somefing we got in common, anyway.

Slight pause.

SANDRA

Hey, can you have visitors? Can you write letters?
Only ... you know, they don't know I'm in here ... like,
I've been in the hospital wing ... I could write Linda.
She could tell our Mum. Yeah, there's Linda. I've got
ever so many friends. You know ... mates. They'll all
be ... you know ... There's Linda ... (She begins to
tick off on her fingers) There's our Linda. She'll be
in ... ah ... ah ... Funny how you can't think when
you're thinking, innit? I lose addresses – that's my
trouble. Yeah, get a real lot of ravers in here. Well, you
know ... like I'm a hairdresser. You meet ever such a
lot of people. Clients. Do their hair. It was great. Best
job I ever had, that. Terry got me in. I was out of a gaff
and his feller give him the chuck. We used to kip in
the basement where they did the colouring ... and a
few other things. No, he was a smashing mate. It was
him give me this cross and chain.

She looks down for it, but it is missing.

SANDRA

Oh. Course ... Fuckin' took it off me when I come in
'ere, didn't they? I've wore it ever since he give it
me. Come in here, it's the first thing they fuckin'
whip. Shan't see that again. He give me a little
mirror with one side enlarged so's you could see your
pores. Dunno what happened to that. Well, moving
around ... I reckon I lost that. Pinched. Something.
He's dead now. (Factual.) Cut his throat.

She fidgets, restless.

SANDRA

Christ my arse is sore! I had twenty-two stitches, you know. I look like a fucking zip. Hey, anybody had the interview?

She looks round, no response.

SANDRA

Fucking old bleeder. Hey did you see that fucking great wart on her neck? Enough to put you right off. She only wants to know all about it. At least with the Old Bill you know where you are. I felt like saying, don't worry about it, whiskers, you're not missing anything. I told her a load of bollocks. Tell her? Dirty bleeder. Fucking lot of shit, they are. All going down though. Writing it all down. Huh! Oh God. Is it hot in here? Only I'm on these tablets to dry me off. God, they don't half make you sweat.

She lifts her arms.

SANDRA

Phew! Like this time they come and took me and our Linda away. You should of seen this bleeder pulling our Linda off the banisters. Oh, upset him. He only had to have a cup of tea next door. Never mind we're left sitting in the meat wagon half an hour. Laugh? They're lice. Maggots. If our Mum had of been there, she'd have sorted them. She don't stand for any of that. How long have we got to wait here for? What the fuck are they all doing in there? As if we didn't know. (Calls) Are you all screwing yourselves?

She looks around, grinning. The smile dies again.

SANDRA

I'm not supposed to be here, anyway, in the first
place. I don't know what I'm doing in nick with all you
lot. I ain't done nothing. If I've told them once I've
said it fifty times what happened. They don't believe
you. You can swear yourself black. Course they've
got it all written down, what you're supposed to have
done. Just because it's different to what I said, one of
us is lying! Well, they ain't going to turn round and
say it's them that's lying. Oh no. It's me. I'm the one
that's lying! Then they get you for that! No, see what
I mean? They get you here in the first place and, if
they find out they've made a mistake, they're gonna
look right fucking idiots saying, oh, we've made a
mistake. She's not supposed to be here … waste of
public money …

She leans around, begging support.

SANDRA

Oh, suit yourselves. Turn the other way. I don't give a
fuck. Load of toms and dippers, you don't have to talk
to me. Makes no fucking difference. Don't put me off
my grub. Listen, the reason I don't eat is because it's
filth, that's why. Nothing to do with you lot. You can
all stuff yourselves.

She hums a tune, and fidgets, restless.

SANDRA

Christ. Sit here all bleeding day. Anybody got the
time? Here, tell you a funny story. Hah! When me
and our littl'un was kids, we only borrowed some old
gink's parrot and went in the parade as Robinson
Crusoe and Man Friday! Laugh! Till I got a belting for

borrowin' one of me Mum's fur coats that is. No, we
only won! We got the prize! Couldn't bleeding believe
it! Up comes this feller. Only wants to take our picture
standing next to the Mayor for the bleeding paper!
Fucking parrot! He's straight off our Linda's arm onto
the Mayor's shoulder! They think it's great. Cameras
going. Taking pictures. All laughing their heads
off! Till he shits a big one down the Mayor's coat. We
pissed ourselves. Soon stopped taking pictures after
that. Couldn't get him out of it quick enough. Poor old
parrot never knew what hit him! Oh, why don't you
all sod off?
Sod off!
Sod off!!

Pause.

SANDRA

Whatever you've done they can't top you for it. Not
anymore. It's against the law. So you don't have to
bother. All I care about is whether ... whether I've
knocked meself up or not. That's all I care about. I
mean, if they told you ... Tell you ... Fucking tell
you anything. How the bloody hell was I supposed
to know? This bloody girl comes round. I don't know
who she was. Some fucking straight. Anyway, I'm not
feeling too good. Next thing I know there's a fucking
doctor. He never done nothing for me. Oh, she says,
you gotta go down this clinic. I thought oh, fuck that.
But no, round she comes, all dressed up in a coat ...
you know the sort. Anyway, I go to this place. It's
miles away. When we get there, it's like a fucking
keep-fit class! It's all a load of rubbish. Worse than
back at school sitting at those desks with nowhere to

put your tits. You're gonna get contractions, she says.
If they told you it fucking hurt, you'd know what they
bloody meant. Bloody women! All lying on the floor
rolling about to music. It was disgusting, you should
have seen some of their legs, like steam rollers. I soon
got out of that. Nothing to do with me. "Tuck your tails
in, Mummies!" Fucking hell. They think you got no
feelings, you know. People see you in a mess you think
they'd … you think they'd … ah … When you're in
real bother you … You can't always act pleasant. Not
when you're worried. Oh no! You gotta toe the fuckin'
line, that's all they care about. Fill in a form. Wait
outside. Stand over there. Who's next? Never mind
I was walking the streets with nowhere to go. Why
should they care? Shut up shop for the night, they're
all right. Little grumble about the train strike. Late
for dinner. It was three days, you know. And nights. I
couldn't think what was happening to me. I went a bit
demented I think. Oh, look the other way, I don't give a
fuck! Makes no difference to me. I hope it rots off. Oh,
course, it couldn't happen to you, could it? Oh no. You
couldn't do a thing like that. Do a thing like that?

Pause.

                    SANDRA
Anyway, there's too many people in the world
already. That's what Terry used to say. One more's
not going to make any difference.

Pause.

                    SANDRA
Could happen to anybody!

Slight pause.

SANDRA

Well he wasn't like a baby. There must have been
something wrong. Babies in prams don't look like
that, they're all clean. Pink. Pleasant-looking. It
was all mottled. Covered in muck. I've never seen
anything so disgusting in my life. After going
through all that. Not as though it ... Anyway, if
there's one thing I can't stand it's babies crying. Well,
it gets on your nerves! He's better off out of it. One less
to worry about. At least it's one off the rates!

Pause.

SANDRA

I mean, it's not as though I'm gonna do it again, is it? I
mean ... is it likely? Last thing I'm gonna do. I'm not a
bloody nutter. Keep pestering you. I don't know what
the fuck I'm doing in here. I haven't done nothing.
I mean, what are they keeping me here for? Do you
know what I think? I think they're keeping us here
on purpose. They want to get you all upset. They've
got it all worked out. (Shouts) you've got it all worked
out, haven't you? I don't care. I don't care. They can
do what they like. Nothing to do with me. None of my
business. Oh no. Oh no.

Slight pause.

She turns her head, and calls off, factually.

SANDRA

Nurse! Nurse, where's my baby? Nurse, could I have
my baby please? Will you bring my baby? Nurse! For
God's sake what have you done with him? Where the
hell is my baby? Now I don't want any more of this
fucking nonsense, you bring me my baby! Nurse?

Give it back! Where is he, you fucking monster, give it
back! Nurse! Mum! Mum! Mummy!

Pause.

SANDRA

Look, is there somebody in there with him? What are
we waiting for? Oh well ... at least it's warm in here.
Shall we have a sing-song?

She looks around.

Then begins to sing to herself, wagging her head, and tapping a
foot.

*Fade to black.*

The End.

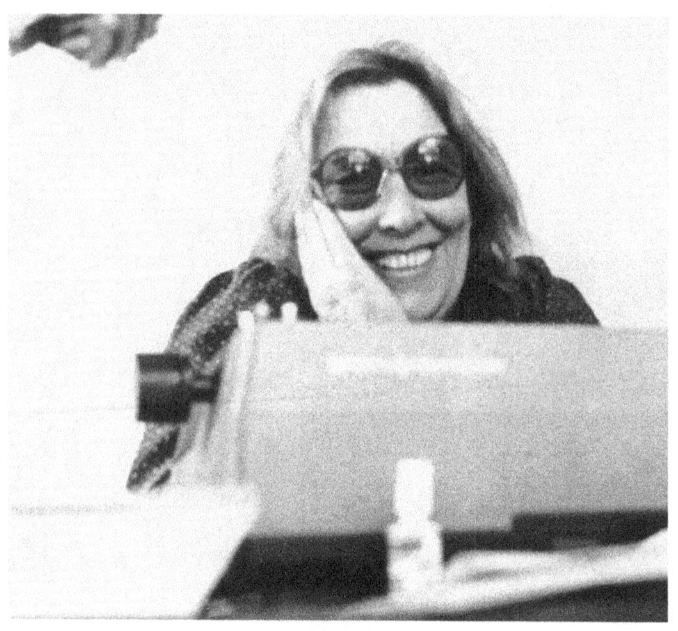

PAM GEMS

1st August 1925 – 13th May 2011

Other plays in print:

| | |
|---|---|
| **CAMILLE** | (Bloomsbury) |
| **DUSA, FISH, STAS and VI** | (Bloomsbury) |
| **MARLENE** | (Bloomsbury) |
| **MRS PAT** | (Bloomsbury) |
| **PIAF** | (Bloomsbury) |
| **QUEEN CHRISTINA** | (Bloomsbury) |
| **THE LADY FROM THE SEA** | (Bloomsbury) |
| **THE LITTLE MERMAID** | (Bloomsbury) |
| **THE SNOW PALACE** | (Bloomsbury) |
| **YERMA** | (Bloomsbury) |
| **STANLEY** | (Nick Hern Books) |
| **THE SEAGULL** | (Nick Hern Books) |
| **UNCLE VANYA** | (Nick Hern Books) |
| **THE CHERRY ORCHARD** | (Cambridge University Press) |

**Bloomsbury**
www.bloomsbury.com

**Nick Hern Books**
www.nickhernbooks.co.uk

**Cambridge University Press**
www.cambridge.org

Q

*website*: www.quotabooks.com
*email*: info@quotabooks.com
Twitter: @Quotabooks